LIVES OF GREAT RELIGIOUS BOOKS

# C. S. Lewis's *Mere Christianity*

## A BIOGRAPHY

## LIVES OF GREAT RELIGIOUS BOOKS

The *Dead Sea Scrolls*, John J. Collins
The *Bhagavad Gita*, Richard H. Davis
John Calvin's *Institutes of the Christian Religion*, Bruce Gordon
The *Book of Mormon*, Paul C. Gutjahr
The Book of *Genesis*, Ronald Hendel
The *Book of Common Prayer*, Alan Jacobs
The Book of *Job*, Mark Larrimore
*The Tibetan Book of the Dead*, Donald S. Lopez, Jr.
C. S. Lewis's *Mere Christianity*, George M. Marsden
Dietrich Bonhoeffer's *Letters and Papers from Prison*, Martin E. Marty
Thomas Aquinas's *Summa theologiae*, Bernard McGinn
The *I Ching*, Richard J. Smith
The *Yoga Sutras of Patanjali*, David Gordon White
Augustine's *Confessions*, Garry Wills

### FORTHCOMING

The Book of *Exodus*, Joel Baden
The Book of *Revelation*, Timothy Beal
Confucius's *Analects*, Annping Chin and Jonathan D. Spence
The *Autobiography* of Saint Teresa of Avila, Carlos Eire
Josephus's *The Jewish War*, Martin Goodman
The *Koran* in English, Bruce Lawrence
The *Lotus Sutra*, Donald S. Lopez, Jr.
Dante's *Divine Comedy*, Joseph Luzzi
The Greatest Translations of All Time: The *Septuagint* and the *Vulgate*,
    Jack Miles
The Passover *Haggadah*, Vanessa Ochs
*The Song of Songs*, Ilana Pardes
The *Daode Jing*, James Robson
Rumi's *Masnavi*, Omid Safi
The *Talmud*, Barry Wimpfheimer

# C. S. Lewis's *Mere Christianity*

## A BIOGRAPHY

George M. Marsden

PRINCETON UNIVERSITY PRESS

*Princeton and Oxford*

Copyright © 2016 by Princeton University Press
Published by Princeton University Press, 41 William Street, Princeton,
New Jersey 08540
In the United Kingdom: Princeton University Press, 6 Oxford Street,
Woodstock, Oxfordshire OX20 1TR

press.princeton.edu

Jacket photograph: Oxford, Addison's Walk, Magdalen College, 1937 /
© The Francis Frith Collection

Library of Congress Cataloging-in-Publication Data

Names: Marsden, George M., 1939–
Title: C.S. Lewis's "Mere Christianity" : a biography / George M. Marsden.
Description: Princeton, NJ : Princeton University Press, 2016. | Series:
Lives of great religious books | Includes bibliographical references and
index.
Identifiers: LCCN 2015021760 | ISBN 9780691153735 (hardcover :
alk. paper)
Subjects: LCSH: Lewis, C. S. (Clive Staples), 1898–1963. Mere
Christianity. | Lewis, C. S. (Clive Staples), 1898–1963—Religion. |
Authors, English—20th century—Biography. | Christianity and
literature.
Classification: LCC PR6023.E926 Z7943 2016 | DDC 230—dc23 LC
record available at http://lccn.loc.gov/2015021760

British Library Cataloging-in-Publication Data is available

This book has been composed in Garamond Premier Pro

Printed on acid-free paper. ∞

Printed in the United States of America

10 9 8 7 6 5 4 3 2

In Memory of Roger Lundin and Christopher W. Mitchell,

Two of My First Guides on This Journey

# CONTENTS

CONTENTS

# C. S. Lewis's *Mere Christianity*

## A BIOGRAPHY

*Mere Christianity* has had a remarkable life story. Most books, even those that make a big splash at the time of publication, eventually fade away like the ripples on a pond. Only a relative few take on lives of their own so that they are generating new ripples even a generation later. Far more rare is a book whose life story tells not only of survival into future generations but even of growing vitality. Such books become classics.

Perhaps it is too early to designate as a classic a book that is only a few generations old. Even so, from the perspective of the early twenty-first century we surely must say that *Mere Christianity* is one of the "great religious books" of the twentieth century, if for no other reason than the phenomenon of its continuing life. A survey of church leaders by the influential American evangelical magazine *Christianity Today* in 2000 ranked it first among the "100 books that had a significant effect on Christians this century."[1] *Time* magazine called Lewis "the hottest theologian of 2005."[2] Since 2001 *Mere Christianity* has sold well over 3.5 million copies in English alone, far more than in the mid-century years after it was first published. Although it has been translated into at least thirty-six languages and has had an untold impact in many parts of the world, including a sizeable readership in China, its most extraordinary popularity has been in the United States. There and elsewhere, fans of the work include Christians from across almost the whole spectrum of denominations, from Roman Catholic and Orthodox to mainline Protestant to evangelical and Pentecostal.

The lasting and even growing appeal of *Mere Christianity* is all the more remarkable in that it was not designed to be a book. C. S. Lewis originally presented it as four separate sets of radio broadcasts that he was asked to deliver for the BBC during the grim days of the Second World War. Lewis edited the talks and published them in three little paperbacks. These enjoyed steady sales in both Great Britain and the United States, helped by C. S. Lewis's popularity as the author of *The Screwtape Letters*. Then in 1952 he combined the three earlier books under the title *Mere Christianity*. The title page specified that this was "a revised and amplified edition, with a new introduction." As a repackaging of earlier works, *Mere Christianity* came out without fanfare or reviews. From these modest beginnings, the book steadily grew in popularity over the decades.

So the question the present volume seeks to answer is this: what is it about this collection of informal radio talks that accounts for their taking on such a thriving life of their own?

The answer to that fascinating question will inevitably have a number of dimensions. First, one has to know something about the author of the book because an author initially gives a book its life. Second, one has to know something about the circumstances under which the book was written, the author's purpose in writing it, and its intended audience. Third, one has to consider how it has been received over the years by differing audiences and communities. What factors in their cultural and religious settings contributed to the book's popularity? What has been its public reception? Who have been its most influential promoters, and how did its influence grow? What have been negative factors and criticisms of the book that point to limitations in its appeal? Finally, taking all these sorts of factors into consideration, what qualities in its character give the book its ongoing "life" or lasting vitality?

Recounting the "life" of a book such as this has some limits. Normally the story of a book after its publication has to do primarily with its public reception. Especially in the case of books that are officially sacred scripture for a particular tradition, the story is largely about differing interpretations or about controversies related to the book. Sometimes a book makes the news if it influences some well-known people, institutions, or major movements. Those matters constitute what might be called the "public life" of a book. *Mere Christianity* does have something of such a public life, and that will be a major topic in the present "biography" of the book. Yet one must keep in mind how much must remain untold. Once it is published, a book such as this takes on a life of its own. Or it might be more accurate to say that it takes on millions of lives as it intersects with the actual lives of its many readers. There is no adequate way to begin to tell about or even to categorize all of these, because readers' reactions doubtless have varied from disgust or disinterest to finding their reading of the book the major turning point in their lives. And everything in between. *Mere Christianity* has been recommended and read—or put aside—by so many people, in so many situations and in so many parts of the world, that it would be impossible even to provide a truly representative sampling of its influences. And then there are untraceable ripple effects from the many whose lives have been changed. One can report types of stories and reactions that have been repeated and seem typical, but these are necessarily impressionistic.

A word about my point of view is in order. I am a great admirer of Lewis and share much of his perspective, but I am not among those who were shaped by *Mere Christianity* at an early age. I have, however, known many impressive Christians whose lives have been changed by this book. I also have been aware of the book's reputation and ongoing popularity. So it seemed a natural candidate for this series. And I thought it would be fascinating to study Lewis, as it has indeed proven to be. Although I write for a university press with high standards of scholarship in mind, I do not see this as a detached academic exercise. As will become apparent from the stories of conflicting appraisals, there is no neutral place to stand in assessing the traits and the impact of a book of this sort. How one depicts the life of such a presentation of the Christian faith will depend largely on where one stands in relation to the sort of faith presented. My stance on that matter is highly sympathetic, even though not uncritical. I am careful to include negative assessments, some of which I share. Yet, as a fellow traveler with Lewis, my overall stance is one of fascination with trying to understand the ongoing vitality of the book—all the more so in light of its imperfections. I think readers from all sorts of points of view can learn from my admittedly sympathetic yet critical exposition. One of my guiding principles has been to write a book about *Mere Christianity* that people who themselves have admired the book can enjoy and from which they can learn.

Lewis's own life has been recounted many times. Readers who are familiar with it may want to skip to chapter 1. Here are the highlights necessary for the present story. Clive Staples Lewis was born in Belfast, Ireland, in 1898. His parents were from the well-to-do professional classes of Protestants on the island bitterly divided by religious factions and on its way to separation in 1922 into the Republic of Ireland and Northern Ireland. C. S. Lewis's mother, Flora Hamilton Lewis, was the daughter of a Church of Ireland clergyman, and his father, Albert James Lewis, was a police court solicitor. The comfortable and secure life enjoyed by Jack, as he became known, and his two-years-older brother, Warnie, was irreparably shattered with the death of their mother from cancer in 1908. The devastated Albert Lewis made matters worse by almost immediately sending his sons off to what became a series of boarding schools. The first of these, Wynyard, in England, was an educational disaster but also was the place where the young Jack began for a time to take with great seriousness the tenets and practices of the Anglican faith in which he had been formally reared. A few years later, when he was between twelve and fourteen and his education was beginning in earnest at an English preparatory school, Malvern College, his faith dissipated into a sea of relativism. First he became intrigued by a multitude of faiths and spiritual outlooks. Then he came to wonder, "In the midst of a thousand such religions stood our own, the thousand and first, labeled True. But on what grounds could I believe this exception?"[3] The culminating step in his pre-university training and in his pilgrimage to confirmed atheism came under the guidance of his rigorous private tutor, William Thompson Kirkpatrick, whom he referred to affectionately in his autobiography as "The Great Knock." Kirkpatrick, the son of a Scottish Presbyterian clergyman, had lost his own faith. He advocated the fashionable dismissal of all religions as cultural adaptations, a position most famously represented in Sir James George Frazer's turn-of-the-century classic study of comparative religions, *The Golden Bough*. Kirkpatrick taught Lewis never to say anything for which he could not offer good reasons.

Lewis moved to Oxford in 1917 to prepare for classical studies there, but he had also enlisted in the military.

Upon completing officer training in Oxford he was sent to France late that year to serve in the deadly trenches of the Great War as a second lieutenant. After several months at the front, he had the good fortune to be wounded just seriously enough to be sent back to England to convalesce. He resumed his Oxford studies early in 1919 and proved to be an outstanding student. By 1923 he had received firsts, or the highest honors, in classical languages, classical philosophy and literature, and English language and literature. Academic jobs were scarce, but in 1924–25 he taught philosophy as a replacement for his former tutor, who was on leave. Then in 1925 he was elected as a fellow, or a don, at Magdalen College, Oxford. Lewis's highest ambition in these early years was to be a poet, and under a pseudonym, Clive Hamilton, he published two books of poetry.

In the meantime, Lewis entered into an unusual domestic arrangement that was both a product of the war and perhaps an expression of freedom from conventionality that was common among the disillusioned young intellectuals and artists of his postwar generation. In the months of preparation for military service, Lewis formed a close friendship with another officer trainee, Paddy Moore. He also became good friends with Moore's mother, Janie, also known as Minto. Mrs. Moore was separated from her husband and in 1917 was forty-five and had a daughter, Maureen, who was then eleven. The eighteen-year-old Lewis visited with the Moores both before and after Paddy left for the front, and he already was expressing considerable affection for Mrs. Moore at that time. Apparently Lewis also made an agreement with Paddy that should one of them die, the other would take care of his dead friend's surviving parent. Paddy did die in the war. And shortly after Lewis arrived back at Oxford at the beginning of 1919, Mrs. Moore and her daughter moved there also to be close to him. Soon Lewis moved in with them, and he continued to live with and take care of Minto until her death in 1951.

No one knows exactly what their early relationship involved, but the preponderance of opinion now inclines toward believing that it was not entirely platonic. That supposition, at least, fits all the known facts. Like Lewis's own mother, Minto was the daughter of a clergyman from Northern Ireland, but unlike Flora Lewis and like the young Jack Lewis, she had lost her faith. So neither Minto nor Jack would have felt restrained by religious principle from a sexual relationship. Lewis later remarked (as an aside in *The Problem of Pain*), "I was as nearly without a moral conscience as a boy could be. . . . Of chastity, truthfulness, and self-sacrifice I thought as a baboon thinks of classical music."[4] Whatever may or may not have been involved, the living arrangements helped put a deep strain on Lewis's relationship with his Victorian father, who was supporting him financially through his student years. Later, when Lewis converted to Christianity, Minto resented it deeply and remained adamantly anti-Christian. Whatever Lewis's relationship with Mrs. Moore during these postconversion years,

Lewis remained dedicated to taking care of her. He also did not seem to entertain a romantic relationship with any other woman so long as she lived.

The centerpiece of Lewis's biography that is most closely related to the story of *Mere Christianity* is the account of his own conversion. Throughout his presentations of the faith, he mentions what he used to think when he was an atheist and then offers considerations that led him to reject that view. As someone who himself had looked at Christianity from the outside and then had been drawn in and enthralled by it, he offers insights drawn from his own pilgrimage from skepticism to commitment. One of the factors that gives authenticity to his presentation is that he is asking others to join him on a journey he has already taken. Lewis himself describes this trek of discovery in his spiritual autobiography, *Surprised by Joy*, and many fine biographers have filled in the details.

Lewis was exactly of that generation of young intellectuals who grew up when the Victorian world was still largely intact, found themselves confronted with the skepticism of modernity, and then were rudely thrust into the excruciating horrors of World War I. Lewis says little in *Surprised by Joy* about the impact of his war experience. But the reality was that of five friends who were with him at officer training school, he was the only one to survive. He later remarked in a letter that the war haunted his dreams for years.[5] While he was at the front, he wrote some bitterly disillusioned poetry:

Come let us curse our Master ere we die,
For all hopes in endless ruins lie,
The good is dead. Let us curse God most high.[6]

After the war, through the 1920s, Lewis struggled to counter the despair inherent in this disillusionment. One thing he shared with many postwar thinkers was a sense that this essentially meaningless war had exploded the nineteenth-century myth of modern progress based on scientific advance. That outlook had provided the rational basis for undermining his faith, but he then found himself deeply dissatisfied with the universe emptied of meaning which that outlook implied. He describes himself as always having been on a quest for "Joy" and as having pangs of desire for some distant beauty. He pursued this quest in his wide study of literature including ancient, classical, Norse, and modern works, as well as in what became his academic specialty: medieval and Renaissance English writers. In the course of his search, a discovery that he said "baptized" his imagination was the magical world of *Phantastes*, by the nineteenth-century maverick Christian writer George MacDonald.

One of Lewis's most illuminating breakthroughs came when his Oxford friend Owen Barfield convinced him of the folly of "chronological snobbery." Lewis defined chronological snobbery as "the uncritical acceptance of the intellectual climate common to our own age and the assumption that whatever has gone out of date is on that account discredited." That insight helped Lewis overcome his naïve acceptance of the latest naturalistic scientific pronouncements that led intellectual snobs such as he had been to dismiss beliefs in spiritual realities as merely "romantic" or "medieval." He saw, rather, that "our own age is also 'a period,' and certainly has, like all periods, its own characteristic illusions."[7] That insight helped him get beyond the shallow modern scientifically based rationalism that had stood as a roadblock to his encountering the spiritual as real.

This was also an era of religious conversions of prominent British literary figures. G. K. Chesterton converted from Anglicanism to Catholicism in 1922. Graham Greene gave up agnosticism for Catholicism in 1926. So did Evelyn Waugh in 1930. The American expatriate T. S. Eliot converted to Anglicanism in 1927. Of these, Chesterton most directly influenced Lewis. Lewis read *The Everlasting Man* not long after it came out in 1925 and "for the first time saw the whole Christian outline of history set out in a form that seemed to me to make sense."[8] Chesterton provided a model for Lewis as an engaging apologist, a novelist, a good-humored stylist, and a learned critic of modern assumptions. Probably reflecting his Northern Irish Protestant heritage, Lewis seems never to have been attracted to the Roman Catholic Church. Yet on his journey toward Christian faith, sophisticated literary Catholics played a pivotal role. By far the most important influence was his friendship with J.R.R. Tolkien, professor of Anglo-Saxon at Oxford. The two met in

1926, found they had much in common in their interests in language and ancient mythologies, and soon became close friends, often sitting up late to discuss common interests.

All these factors converged toward leading Lewis step by step toward Christian belief. His own literary studies played a role. As a specialist in early English literature, he spent much of his time reading and analyzing great Christian writers. He compared these with acclaimed skeptical writers such as Voltaire, Edward Gibbon, George Bernard Shaw, or H. G. Wells, with whom he should have sympathized, but they "all seemed a little thin."[9] One important step was an incident in his college room early in 1926, when "the hardest boiled of all the atheists I ever knew" remarked that the Gospels looked surprisingly reliable as historical records and that it almost seemed as though what they said about the Dying God was something that "had really happened once."[10] On a totally different front, Lewis admired Plato and for a time was much attracted to modern idealist philosophy, which offered an alternative to the growing materialism of the age. Yet all this still left him with a sense that there was something more. Then everything began to fall into place. Lewis remarks in a famous passage from *Surprised by Joy* that "amiable agnostics will talk cheerfully about 'man's search for God.' To me, as I then was, they might as well have talked about the mouse's search for the cat."[11] He also described his experience "as if I were a man of snow beginning to melt," an image he used again most effectively in *The Lion, the Witch, and the Wardrobe*, where the snow melting marked the breaking of the witch's spell and signaled the return of the lion Aslan.[12]

The first step in the process, probably in the spring of 1930,[13] involved Lewis's coming to accept theism and beginning to attend Christian services at his college and at the local Anglican parish. Yet, like many modern Christians of the time, he did not believe in the divinity of Christ and the doctrines of salvation that flowed from it. The second step took place as the direct result of a late-night conversation on September 19, 1931, with Tolkien and another Christian academic friend, Hugh Dyson. The three dined at Magdalen College and then took a stroll around Addison's Walk, a picturesque streamside path on the college grounds, discussing the nature of myth. They moved to Lewis's rooms, where the topic turned to Christianity in a conversation that went until 3:00 a.m. Tolkien was instrumental in convincing Lewis that Christianity could be a "true myth." Lewis's conversion to theism had been largely on rational grounds. Myths went further in speaking to humans' deepest longings. As a broadly Christian theist, Lewis had admired Jesus as a great teacher and example. Soon after his conversation with Tolkien and Dyson, he found himself believing in the stupendous life-reorienting reality that Jesus Christ was God incarnate. As he explained in a letter to his lifelong friend and confidant, Arthur Greeves, "The story of Christ is simply a true myth: a myth working on us in the same way as the others, but with this tremendous difference that *it really happened.*"[14]

Lewis very soon took up the task of attempting to share with others his journey of discovery. During the fall of 1932 he wrote his first prose book, *The Pilgrim's Regress*. Presented as a modern version of John Bunyan's *Pilgrim's Progress*, it is sometimes an obscure allegory of his intellectual travels and seems written for other intellectuals. Lewis's pilgrim, John, sets out to find a distant island representing the human desire for "Joy." On the way, John is captured by a giant called "The Spirit of the Age," who, like modern science, claims to see through everything to its true essence. John is rescued by Reason. He meets "Mother Kirk," who represents traditional Christianity, or what he later calls "mere Christianity," and offers the only way over the great canyon between him and his desired destination. He attempts the long way around and meets representations of all sorts of the false hopes offered by ancient and modern philosophies, such as humanism, Enlightenment, nihilism, idealism, modern art, and modernized religion. Reason helps lead him back to Mother Kirk, who leads him to the island of his dream. On his return journey, or "regress," John understands how different everything looks and how inadequate are the once-tempting philosophies now that he has seen "the real shape of the world we live in" and the true human condition "on a knife-edge between Heaven and Hell."[15]

During the 1930s, Lewis's principal activities continued to be those of an Oxford don. They involved a great deal of tutoring of students in medieval and early English literature. Lewis also became one of the most popular lecturers at the university. And in 1935 he published his first academic book, *The Allegory of Love*, a study of ideals of courtly love in medieval literature.

One of the most significant developments for Lewis in the 1930s was the expansion of his friendship with Tolkien into an informal literary group that eventually became known as "The Inklings." This was a group of friends who met each Thursday evening in Lewis's rooms at Magdalen College to discuss each other's work. In addition to Lewis and Tolkien, the fellowship included Hugo Dyson, Nevill Coghill, Dr. R. E. Harvard, Owen Barfield (when he was in town), Warnie Lewis, and others. During World War II, when Oxford University Press had moved to Oxford, the novelist Charles Williams became a member especially valued by Lewis. Sometimes on Tuesday mornings the group met less formally for beer and talk at The Eagle and Child, a local pub. Tolkien read chapters of what became *The Lord of the Rings* to this group.

Lewis tried out his works on these friends. By the later 1930s he was looking for more popular ways to present the Christian message. One way he did so was by writing a space-travel novel, *Out of the Silent Planet* (1938). In it he shows how earth and especially the false hopes of scientism look from the perspective of a planet, Malacandra, ruled by creatures still in harmony with the music of the spheres. Earth, in contrast, is the "silent planet" because it is ruled by an intelligence, Satan, who has rebelled against God and hence is out of harmony with the good and the beautiful. Lewis represents the reigning human spirit in the character of the scientist Weston, who is obsessed with using technical power to rule the universe but is thereby blinded from understanding the higher intelligence and the moral beauty of the supposedly "primitive" creatures he encounters on Malacandra.

Then, in the summer of 1939, at the request of a publisher of a series of books for Christian laypeople, Lewis embarked on his first straightforward defense of basic orthodox Christianity, *The Problem of Pain*. "Not many years ago, when I was an atheist," he began in its first sentence. He then explained why he, like so many who had come of age around the time of the Great War, had come to believe that this vast universe, as described by modern science and populated with creatures capable of such great evil, must be empty of meaning. "Either there is no spirit behind the universe, or else a spirit indifferent to good and evil, or else an evil spirit." Yet he had come to realize that the common experiences of humanity pointed to a universe in which the historical events at the center of Christianity provided a compelling account that had the ring of truth. In arguments that anticipated many of those of *Mere Christianity*, he went on to explain how the possibility of pain was compatible with an omnipotent God who created a universe with creatures who were genuinely free to resist God's love. Christian teachings regarding the fall of humans, the possibly redemptive uses of pain, the promise of Heaven, and even the threat of Hell all fit with human experience, common sense, and a sense of justice.[16]

Lewis's domestic situation had also been evolving. His brother, Warnie, who had had his own conversion experience in 1930, aided in the purchase of a substantial house, The Kilns, near Oxford, which had a very attractive garden, pond, and woods. Mrs. Moore was the legal owner of the property, but the Lewis brothers had rights to live there for life. In 1932 Warnie retired from the army and moved in permanently. He was a great asset in his brother's work, aiding him in matters such as correspondence, but also suffered from serious bouts with alcoholism. Minto's daughter, Maureen, who studied and then taught music at a local school, remained in the household until she was married in 1940.

Then, on September 1, 1939, Hitler's armies invaded Poland, and two days later England and France declared war on Germany. Warnie, a career officer, was immediately called to active service. Many schoolchildren were also immediately evacuated from London in expectation of German air raids. Mrs. Moore opened their home to four girls, the first of numbers of such children who would be staying there during the war years. Jack Lewis, who would not pass age forty until November, also feared being called up. During the rest of 1939 and into early 1940, there was an ominous lull. Then in April Hitler invaded Norway and Denmark, and in May he marched through the Low Countries toward Paris. The allied French and British armies were helpless to stop the onslaught. If it had not been apparent previously, the very survival of an independent Great Britain was at stake. Lewis would not be called up, but in these trying times he would find ways to serve on other fronts.

# War Service

Those of us who have not lived through the horrors of warfare can hardly imagine the prolonged fears, anger, sufferings, sorrows, and uncertainties that many English people endured during the bleakest years of World War II. Americans might think of the shock and outrage that they experienced in reaction to the 9/11 attacks and then consider the appalling number of times such feelings would have to be multiplied even to begin to compare them to those experienced due to the traumas of the Blitz on London and other cities. Between September 1940 and May 1941, the German Luftwaffe poured bombs on London seventy-one times, killing over twenty thousand citizens and seriously injuring tens of thousands more. At one point the relentless pounding went on fifty-seven nights in a row. Casualties often numbered over a thousand on the worst nights in London. Devastating attacks struck fifteen other British industrial cities, leaving some, most memorably Coventry, in almost total ruin. Nearly twenty thousand civilians perished in these outlying areas, and vastly many more suffered overwhelming personal losses. People spent their nights in excruciating terror agonizing about their own safety or the fate of their children and loved ones. And throughout the British Isles, countless numbers woke up each morning trying to suppress the dread that that might the day when there would be a knock at the door to deliver the message that their beloved son, grandson, or husband would never come home again.

Distressing personal anxieties were magnified in these early years by the real danger of invasion and defeat. Hitler had already exhibited many of his demonic qualities. The British leadership expected an invasion, and indeed he was planning one. A German victory would mean the end of free British civilization as it had been known in the island kingdom. During the six weeks after Hitler's armies suddenly swept through Belgium, the Netherlands, and Luxembourg in May 1940, the unthinkable happened. Until this point this new war with Germany had seemed like a continuation of the first Great War. As C. S. Lewis wrote to his lifelong friend Arthur Greeves, one had a "ghostly feeling that it has all happened before—that one fell asleep during the last war and had a delightful dream and has now waked up again."[1] A similar sense that this second war would be a continuation of the first was also present among the high command. Winston Churchill relates in his memoirs that in 1940 it was natural to regard the French, who had endured the brunt of "the terrible land fighting of 1914–1918," as having the "primacy in the military art."[2] The unthinkable was that this mighty French army with its British allies, which so recently had stood strong for four years, could now be completely routed in a few weeks. The British army escaped the Germans in late May and early June only through the amazingly improvised rescue from Dunkirk. In a memorable speech, Prime Minister Churchill promised, "We shall fight" from the beaches to the hills if necessary, but would never surrender. The speech was so powerful because the possibility was so real.[3]

For most of the next year, the British people struggled to cope with a combination of the immediate terrors of blitz bombing, the loss of loved ones, the dread of losing others, and fears of a German invasion. Shortages, rationing, blackouts, Home Guard patrols, and displaced people were constant reminders of extreme and dangerous times. Many British people were undergoing in the space of months a range of intensity of experiences that normally might take a lifetime to unfold.

Oxford was considered relatively safe from the bombings, but the early part of the war was nonetheless grim. C. S. Lewis, according to his friend and physician, Dr. Robert Havard, was greatly disheartened by the outbreak of the war. In addition to experiencing the distresses shared with most people, Lewis was pained to think that he had for so many years prepared himself to write and now, just when he was coming into his own, the war might limit his freedom to do that. During the dark days of July 1940, Lewis closed a letter to a friend with "Well: we are on the very brink of the abyss now. Perhaps we shan't be meeting again in this world. In case we don't, good bye and God bless you." He added a postscript that he realized he was being melodramatic.[4] Havard, who was also one of the Inklings, reports that after the fall of France they spent a depressing evening speculating on which of their writings the Nazis might find offensive if there were an occupation. Lewis recalled that in *The Pilgrim's Regress* he had depicted dwarfs of "a black kind with shirts," though most his writings were not political enough to be attacked.[5]

Lewis's own bit of military service came from joining the Home Guard, made up of men not involved in the regular service who would be prepared to help resist a possible German invasion. His duties involved patrolling the streets of Oxford all night once a week. Sometimes he found the nighttime walks beautiful, and he enjoyed talking to men from ordinary ranks of society. He reported one working man remarking (in an analogy to sports matches) about the expected invasion, "Well, it looks as if we are for the Final and that it will be on the home ground."[6] He also sometimes got to try out his apologetic arguments on (literally) the man on the street. He reported in October 1940 that he had "succeeded in making my . . . fellow sentry realize for the first time in his life that 'nature' can't have 'purposes' unless it is a rational substance, and if it is you'd better call it God, or the gods, or a god, or the devil."[7]

England was still suffering when, on February 7, 1941, the Reverend J. W. Welch, director of the Religious Broadcasting Department of the BBC, wrote what would prove to be a momentous letter to C. S. Lewis. While immediate invasion seemed less likely, the devastating bombing was continuing. By that time, the imposing BBC building, Broadcasting House, in the heart of London, had been hit by bombs on two occasions, once when they could be heard during a broadcast. It was from the roof of that building that Edward R. Murrow made his famous eyewitness reports describing the Blitz to American audiences. Welch was situated in Bristol, where he also had a narrow escape as bombs were falling during a Sunday-evening religious broadcast. Welch had never met C. S. Lewis, but he had been greatly impressed by the Oxford don's recent and timely apologetic work, *The Problem of Pain*. He thanked Lewis for that book and asked him if he might be willing to help with religious broadcasting. "The microphone," Welch explained, "is a limiting and often irritating instrument, but the quality of thinking and the depth of conviction which I find in your book ought surely to be shared with a great many other people; and for any talk we can be sure of a fairly intelligent audience of more than a million."[8]

That what turned out to be such a fruitful proposal should come from an official of the BBC calls for some explanation and background. The British Broadcasting Corporation was a noncommercial company serving the British public under a royal charter. The company had an explicitly Christian dimension. Broadcasting House, completed in 1931, was inscribed with a dedication to "the almighty God" and with a prayer that its work might promote whatever might lead hearers to "tread the path of wisdom and righteousness."[9] Those sentiments reflected the outlook of the BBC's founding director general, Sir John Reith, a deeply religious Scotsman who presided until 1938. Reith was determined that the new medium should be used not just for entertainment but for edifying public service. Under Reith's leadership the BBC broadcast daily religious services, meditations, and music during the week and included church services and other Christian programming on Sundays. In deference to the nation's formal Christian heritage, secular programming on Sundays had to be tasteful, excluding jazz or frivolous comedy or variety shows.[10]

The war brought some changes to such policies. For the sake of the troops, the BBC began broadcasting variety shows (not live, only repeats), dance music, and sports in its Forces Programme on Sundays, which anyone could tune to. The war also forced the BBC to limit its domestic broadcasting to a single frequency, so it was virtually the voice of the nation. For James Welch the problem was how to make religious broadcasting both suitable and competitive in this new and trying situation. In April 1940 he personally visited the troops in France, where he confirmed what he and other Christian leaders were all too aware of already:

CHAPTER ONE

that there was a huge gap between Great Britain's formal public recognition of Christianity and its actual practice among the British people. Welch estimated that two-thirds of BBC listeners lived without any reference to God. One survey of British army recruits revealed that only 23 percent knew the meaning of Easter.[11] In that setting, conventional religious broadcasts were not going to touch most listeners. Radios had to warm up, and during the war many people kept their radios dialed in at low volume in order to hear news bulletins or alerts. The challenge was to get them to turn the volume up. One format that was working in other departments of the BBC was that of the informative talk. Experts might talk on gardening or how to prepare meals under the restrictions of food rationing. Welch had already tried such formats for religious broadcasts. He also recognized the advantage in a speaker who was a layperson and not professionally religious.

The war made it extraordinarily difficult to strike the right balance in religious broadcasting. Welch was very eager to serve the war effort, but like other BBC officials, he was determined to retain the agency's independence and not let themselves be pawns used for state propaganda. Such freedom, they maintained, was one of the central differences between Great Britain and totalitarian states such as Nazi Germany or the U.S.S.R. Yet, at the same time, they had to adhere to some wartime restrictions and also take into account the extenuating circumstances of all-out war for survival. So, for instance, after the fall of France, when invasion seemed imminent, the BBC governors banned pacifists from speaking on any subject. Welch protested strongly and repeatedly and even considered resigning over the issue. Although he was not a pacifist himself, he believed that hearing from them would help remind people that war involved moral choices.[12]

The war also accentuated the ongoing problem of who should be represented in religious broadcasting. The general policy was not to include extremists. So the BBC did not offer broadcasting time to representatives of fundamentalist or other nonmainstream sects. And atheists on the left often protested against the explicitly Christian outlook of the programming. Even so, it was an extraordinary challenge to represent all the major nonextreme religious viewpoints on a single national network. Welch himself was an Anglican. In England somewhat over half the population was Anglican by formal baptism, but the great majority of those were only nominally churched. The free churches, such as the Methodist or Baptist churches, accounted for perhaps another 15 percent. Roman Catholics counted only for about 7 percent, but they, like free church members, were more likely to be active.[13] The challenge was to create interest among these groups without controversy. That was becoming increasingly difficult during the war. For instance, William Temple, bishop of York (who became archbishop of Canterbury in 1942), was a friend of Welch and a regular speaker on the BBC. But Temple's progressive social views (published in 1942 in his very popular *Christianity and the Social Order*) brought an outcry from conservatives that religion was being used for partisan political purposes. By mid-1941 the BBC had arrived at a policy that religious speakers should not pontificate on the specifics of economic and political matters on which they had no real expertise. And speakers with competence should state on the air that they were speaking as experts and acknowledge when their views were controversial.[14]

In such a setting, C. S. Lewis must have seemed like a godsend. Lewis was a literary scholar with no discernible political interests. The fact was that he rarely even listened to the radio or closely followed the news.[15] Yet, as the author of a space-travel fantasy as well as the generalist's account *The Problem of Pain*, he apparently had an interest in reaching wider audiences. Welch's first suggestion was "You might speak about the Christian, or lack of Christian, assumptions underlying modern literature" and then move "from description and analysis to something more positive and helpful." That was a thoroughly safe proposal that might draw on Lewis's expertise as a professor of literature. Welch's second suggestion, related to what was the genesis of *Mere Christianity*, was that Lewis offer "series of talks on something like 'The Christian Faith As I see It—by a Layman': I am sure there is a need of a positive restatement of Christian doctrine in lay language."[16]

Lewis responded on February 10 to say that he would like to do some broadcasts. "Modern literature," he said, "would not suit me." Rather, he already had worked out a definite idea of where to begin a presentation of the basics of Christianity for a modern audience. He would talk mainly about "the Law of Nature, or objective right and wrong." Lewis explained that the New Testament "by preaching repentance and forgiveness, always *assumes* an audience who already believe in the Law of Nature and know they have disobeyed it." One could not assume such sensibilities any more in modern England, "and therefore most apologetic begins a stage too far on." So his "first step" would be "to create, or recover, the sense of guilt." Accordingly, he planned not to mention Christianity until the end of the series, "and would prefer not to unmask my battery till then." For the title of the series he suggested "'The Art of being Shocked'" or perhaps "'These Humans.'"[17]

Lewis was acutely aware that Great Britain was a Christian country in name only. That disparity was all the more troubling because the war had brought with it a good bit of talk about fighting for "Christian civilization." Yet there was little clarity, let alone agreement, on what that might mean.[18] Christianity was invoked on ceremonial occasions, and there was some token Christian teaching and observance in the schools. Christianity still had some public privilege, as the BBC broadcasts themselves illustrated. Yet at every level of society, and especially among the intellectuals and the working classes, the most common assumption was that traditional Christianity was out of date and unscientific. The left-wing writer George Orwell captured the spirit of the times when he wrote in 1940, "We have got to be children of God, even though the God of the Prayer-book no longer exists."[19]

In February 1941, Lewis was at a moment when a request to venture into popular broadcasting fit remarkably well with what else he was doing. The war and the draft had reduced the student population at Oxford and thus relieved him of some of the task of tutoring, which was his principal duty as a don. He was still immensely busy, but that was largely because he was constantly taking on new assignments in addition to his voluminous reading and other academic work. He also was on the lookout for edifying nonacademic projects. The latest had come as an inspiration during the darkest part of the war, when evil was in the air and German invasion seemed imminent. While sitting in church in July 1940, Lewis conceived the idea of a series of letters, originally to be titled *As One Devil to Another*, which would be from a senior devil to a novice. As in *Out of the Silent Planet*, he would try to provide fresh insight on the human condition by viewing it from an unexpected perspective. The subject would be an individual's Christian faith, and the book would draw on Lewis's own struggles during his conversion experience. The novice devil would be trying to thwart the incipient faith of a "patient" to whom he had been assigned but would often be botching the job, much to the chagrin of his mentor. Lewis found it easy to write what became *The Screwtape Letters* and probably had the book finished by the end of 1940.[20] The letters were published in thirty-one weekly installments in an Anglican magazine, *The Guardian*, between May and November 1941.

Once James Welch received Lewis's positive response to his inquiry, he turned the arrangements for the radio talks over to his colleague the Reverend Eric Fenn, the BBC's assistant head of religious broadcasting. Fenn, a Presbyterian, had refused military service as a pacifist during World War I. He was knowledgeable as a theologian, and he later taught Christian doctrine at a theological college. [21] Fenn suggested a series of four live broadcasts in August and met with Lewis in Oxford to discuss them.

Coincidentally, Lewis had recently been enlisted by the secret Military Intelligence to record a talk to be broadcast in Iceland on the cultural affinities between Britain and Iceland evidenced in Norse literature. Iceland was an important staging ground for the British forces whose continued presence there depended on the good will of the Icelandic people. Lewis seems to have kept quiet about his work with Military Intelligence but he apparently alluded to the recording it in a letter to Arthur Greeves in which he said he had recently heard a recording of himself, and "I was unprepared for the total unfamiliarity of the voice."[22] Lewis was a most popular lecturer at Oxford, and his radio voice was remarkably effective, with clearly an educated accent but enough of the touch of his Irish origins not to sound stuffy.

During the months prior to the August broadcasts Lewis took on another project that allowed him to serve the war effort directly in his new role as Christian apologist and evangelist and also to hone his skills in communicating with general audiences. Not long after the BBC request, the chaplain-in-chief of the Royal Air Force (RAF) asked Lewis if he would serve as a traveling lecturer to RAF units. Though Lewis did not like to travel, especially in wartime conditions, often on freezing and unlit trains, he saw the opportunity as a duty and readily accepted.

During the Battle of Britain of 1940 and 1941, the RAF was *the* linchpin to defense of the British Isles and Britain's counterattack against Germany. "Never in the field of human conflict was so much owed by so many to so few," Prime Minister Churchill famously remarked to the House of Commons in August 1940. The RAF attracted some of the nation's best and brightest, but its ranks included many ordinary young men eager to serve their country. Among those who were on flying crews, the mortality rate was appalling. Stuart Barton Babbage, a chaplain who hosted Lewis one weekend in 1941, recounts that at his base at Norfolk, "the grim fact was that, on the average, a man only completed thirteen raids before being killed or posted missing." The chances of surviving the prescribed service of two tours of thirty sorties each were minimal. As a chaplain, Babbage often met with frightened young men in the prime of life who "desperately wanted to live and to know what it is to love and be loved."[23]

In May 1941 Lewis wrote to his friend Sister Penelope, an Anglican nun, "I've given some talks to the R. A. F. at Abingdon already and as far as I can judge they were a complete failure." The job was one of those "one dare neither refuse nor perform." He took comfort in the Old Testament story that God had used an ass to convert the prophet Balaam. At the bottom of the letter he sketched a picture of a donkey wearing a mortarboard next to a nun outside a stable in the radiance of the heavenly city.[24] Lewis soon encountered some greater successes, and throughout the war he continued his arduous "missionary journies" (as he put it to Dorothy Sayers)[25] to RAF bases. In 1941, having spent all of his summer vacation going on two- or three-day trips to RAF bases, he wrote, "I had never realized how tiring perpetual traveling is (specially on crowded trains),"[26] Chaplain Babbage thought that he was effective, even if the circumstances were trying. At Norfolk Lewis had to speak in the open air to Sunday-morning "parade services" that Lewis thought, by being required, were designed to "harden men in impenitence."[27] Voluntary evening meetings had the drawback that men faced peer pressure against leaving the barracks for a religious meeting. Nonetheless, the RAF talks helped the radio talks by giving Lewis valuable experience and feedback from addressing people from many ranks of society.

Lewis later reflected on lessons he learned from these encounters. For instance, he learned that materialism was not the only major competitor to Christian faith. Many English people were open to alternative religious outlooks such as Theosophy, Spiritualism, or British Israelitism. Furthermore, working-class people tended to be entirely skeptical about the relevance of anything historical, and often they had heard in a general way that textual criticism had cast doubt on Scripture. Lewis also learned not only not to use hard words but also that some ordinary words differ in meaning to the uneducated and the educated. For instance, "*creature* means not creature but 'animal.'" Or "*Morality*, nearly always means 'chastity.'" He thought the educated speaker simply needs to learn the popular English language, "just as a missionary learns Bantu before preaching to the Bantus." So the evangelist or apologist needs to be first a translator. Beyond that, he said, "the greatest barrier I have met is the almost total absence from the minds of my audience of any sense of sin."[28]

Addressing a general radio audience had its own challenges. Lewis had to imagine the immense range of varieties of people who might be listening in and then think of ways to engage and hold their attention. Imagination was, of course, one of Lewis's strong suits. Despite being an Oxford don, he seems from the beginning to have been good at picturing all the varieties of people who might be tuned in and what it would take to communicate to such diverse audiences. What might they have in common? Most would not be much interested in hearing about Christianity, especially not initially. In his May 1941 letter to Sister Penelope, Lewis provided an additional encapsulation of his earliest conception of his first series of radio talks.

Sister Penelope was an accomplished writer herself and had become something of a spiritual confidante of Lewis after she had written to him in appreciation of *Out of the Silent Planet*. Apparently she was working on some talks as well, and he thought they should get together to compare notes. "Mine," Lewis explained, "are *praeparatio evangelica*, rather than *evangelium*, and attempt to convince people that there is a moral law, that we disobey it, and that the existence of a Law-giver is at least very probable and also (*unless* you add the Christian doctrine of the Atonement) imparts despair rather than comfort."[29] In his view, the lack of a sense of sin was the number-one barrier. But even in post-Christian Great Britain, people had some common moral sensibilities.

The talks had to be prepared well in advance for approval by Eric Fenn and then to be cleared by the censor. There was no room for ad lib. They also had to be an exact length to fit the time slot. The German propagandist Lord Haw-Haw, broadcasting on the same wavelength, could fill any unexpected silences in a broadcast. Wartime sensibilities could be delicate. For instance, someone at the BBC criticized an early title for the series, "Inside Information," as "rather unseemly."[30] Lewis would have to take the train to London to do the live broadcasts. When he accepted the assignment, England was still in the midst of the Blitz, so he had also accepted that danger as a matter of course. By August, to his great relief, the nightly bombing had stopped.

# Broadcast Talks

Lewis delivered the first of his talks from Broadcasting House on Wednesday, August 6, 1941, from 7:45 to 8:00 p.m. That might sound like prime time, but it was not. The preceding program was fifteen minutes of news broadcast in Norwegian to Nazi-occupied Norway. And few listeners would have been tuning in to catch the beginning of the next program: songs from a Welsh cultural festival.[1]

Eric Fenn was highly pleased with Lewis's first broadcast, and gradually the BBC made the time slots much more favorable. Justin Phillips, who as head of heritage for the BBC later wrote a carefully documented account of the broadcasts, *C. S. Lewis in a Time of War*, provides an astute expert's account of the tone of Lewis's presentations, based on the texts and the surviving recording. "He carries you along," writes Phillips, "as a good companion walking down a road. It is like listening to a benevolent uncle trying to explain the laws of cricket to his nephew." Lewis comes across as ever the good teacher, who, while presenting arguments, does so with a sense of personal contact, engaging the spirit as much as the mind. He "leaves you in no doubt that he believes what he is saying with passion." Without being patronizing, he attempts to lead people gently toward new avenues of thought.

Many did not listen, and some were repelled, but one recollection from Lewis's friend and biographer, George Sayers, testifies to Lewis's power to communicate. Sayers recalls being in a pub filled with soldiers one Wednesday evening. "At a quarter to eight, the bartender turned the radio up for Lewis. 'You listen to this bloke,' he shouted: 'He's really worth listening to.' And those soldiers did listen attentively for the entire fifteen minutes."[2]

From the outset Lewis adopted an informal "I" and "you" stance and talked about shared experiences, suggesting that he was not so different from his listeners. "Every one has heard people quarreling," he began. He went on to depict very ordinary arguments over a seat, a place in line, sharing a bit of orange, or keeping a promise, all the sort of things familiar to everyone, "educated people as well as uneducated, children as well as grownups." From there he began to develop a substantial argument, but always moving the listener along in small steps. Each step involves logic, but it is typically a logic of persuasion appealing to experience, not a philosopher's strict demonstration. Everyone believes in right and wrong as objective realities. And if there is an actual moral "Law of Nature," that, in turn, is best

CHAPTER TWO

explained by the existence of a personality who has designed the universe and cares about right and wrong. Yet the controlling power outside the universe could not be one of the facts inside the universe, "no more than the operator of a cinema could appear on the screen." In the published versions, Lewis changed that to "no more than the architect of a house could actually be a wall or staircase or fireplace in that house."[3]

Only in the last minutes of the fourth talk did Lewis get to explaining very briefly how traditional Christianity is the solution that fits these clues to the meaning of the universe. But even if the Gospel promise that "God Himself becomes a man to save man from the disapproval of God" is ultimately "a thing of unspeakable comfort," it involves first facing some "terrifying facts." (As he would later say of Aslan in *Narnia*, Christianity is not "safe.") If the universe includes real evil that needs to be condemned and fought against, we cannot exempt ourselves from such judgments. Before we get comfort, we must face truth. Unlike the usual religious radio talk, Lewis's did not end on sweet notes of sentiment, piety, hope, and self-improvement.[4]

The broadcasts drew a stack of mail. Due to a postponement, the BBC found a time for a fifth talk, and Lewis agreed to use that for answering questions from listeners. When that program was aired on September 6, it was in a highly favorable time slot on a Saturday evening rather than a Wednesday. Lewis's talk followed a popular comedy program and preceded a review of the second year of the war, *No Longer Alone*, thus guaranteeing a multimillion audience.[5] Lewis used the opportunity of this fifth talk (in the published versions, it is chapter 2, "Some Objections") to elaborate on the argument that an objective moral law is a more convincing explanation of our experience than is an evolutionary account that says our sense of right and wrong is "herd instinct" or "just a moral convention." In one of his relatively few direct references to the war, he also made explicit what was the most compelling implication of talking about actual right and wrong in England in 1941: "If no set of moral ideas was truer or better than any other, there would be no sense in preferring civilized morality to savage morality, or Christian morality to Nazi morality."[6]

The BBC executives knew they had a winner. On September 4, 1941, two days before the fifth broadcast, Fenn wrote to Lewis with his request for a second series, suggesting that these talks be broadcast on five Sunday afternoons between 4:45 and 5:00 p.m. in January and February. The topic, Fenn suggested, would be "What Christians Believe." Fenn, who was the editor for all of the broadcasts, may even have been the originator of the idea that became book 2 of *Mere Christianity*. It seems more likely, though, that because Fenn and Lewis had been seeing each other for most of the broadcasts, they had already talked of this possibility and topic. Lewis immediately replied with a note saying, "I'll take the job."[7]

In Lewis's brief note he also thanked Fenn for help in making arrangements for another revealing part of the enterprise. He had asked that the small fees he received for his talks be distributed to widows and orphans. Lewis had already been doing this with the payments he had been receiving for the serialization of *The Screwtape Letters*, which had been appearing weekly in the *Guardian* since May. Soon, as a suddenly well-known speaker and author, he would be adding substantial book royalties to his charitable contributions. A number of his letters suggested specific persons or groups to whom the money should go. By the next year he would be hit with an unexpected and very large tax bill, because British law did not provide for tax deductions for charitable contributions. Lewis would have to have his friend, Owen Barfield, an attorney, set up a charitable trust to which Lewis could channel his fees and royalties, thus guaranteeing that he would not be undertaking his additional work as a popular Christian advocate for any personal financial gain.[8]

Speaking on the radio involved a larger personal cost. Lewis received "an enormous pile of letters from strangers." Some, he said were "from lunatics who sign themselves 'Jehovah' or begin 'Dear Mr. Lewis I was married at age 20 to a man I didn't love,'" but most were serious inquiries that he answered fully and conscientiously.[9] Eventually he enlisted his brother, Warnie, to type letters and answer routine correspondence. Over the years, Jack made time, often by rising early, to reply to thousands of letters. He also honored requests for prayers, and so he worried that his prayer lists had become too long.[10] Many of the early letters asked for transcripts of talks. That helped impel Lewis to seek to have them published. By October he had an agreement with the publisher Geoffrey Bles for a small volume that would be called simply *Broadcast Talks* and include the first set of talks plus the five new ones. In the meantime, the letters kept coming. In February he complained to Eric Fenn that he had written thirty-five letters the previous day, "all out of working hours of course," and said, "'It gets one down.'" He wished that the talks could have been published in the BBC paper, *The Listener*. That way many letters would have gone to the paper rather than to Lewis directly, and no one would have had to ask for copies of the talks.[11]

In preparing for the second set of talks, "What Christians Believe," Lewis took the significant step of trying to ensure that what he would say would represent what he would later call "mere Christianity." He wanted to be sure that he would not be taking sides on any matter of dispute among orthodox believers of the major Christian groups. So he sent drafts of the talks not only to Fenn, an ordained Presbyterian, but also to three other clergymen, one of the Church of England, one Roman Catholic, and one "dissenting." The dissenter was a Methodist, the Reverend Joseph Dowell, who was an RAF chaplain with whom Lewis had become friends. Lewis explained that he was "anxious to include nothing that all Christians do not agree on."[12] The Catholic was Dom Bede Griffiths, and the representative of the Church of England was probably the Reverend Dr. Austin Farrer, an Oxford theologian and friend.[13]

Lewis's introduction to the radio talks anticipated some of the themes that would appear in the influential longer introduction to *Mere Christianity*, although he did not use that term. He began: "It's not because I'm anyone in particular that I've been asked to tell you what Christians believe." Rather he was speaking as a layperson who had recently been converted to Christianity, and he knew some of the difficulties the faith presented to unbelievers and how it looked from the outside. Otherwise he was an "amateur" and a "beginner," not a professional. That was why he had circulated the manuscripts among the four professionals. Even if they each said some things differently, they all affirmed that "the greater part of it is what all Christians agree on." Admittedly there are unfortunate differences among Christians, but that should not distract from large areas of agreement that are "big enough to blow any of us sky-high if it happens to be true." To refuse to listen because of the differences would be "as if a man bleeding to death refused medical assistance because he'd heard that some doctors differed about the treatment of cancer."[14]

When Eric Fenn read Lewis's drafts of these talks in early December, he recognized that he was seeing something extraordinary. One should be reminded that this response was coming from a sharp editorial professional who had dealt with virtually every BBC religious broadcast of recent years. "I have at last had time today to read your scripts," he wrote to Lewis. "I think they are quite first class—indeed I don't know when I have read anything in the same class at all. There is a clarity and inexorableness about them, which made me positively gasp."[15]

Eric Fenn would eventually be joined by countless others in finding this brief set of five talks, what became book 2 of *Mere Christianity*, compelling. They are, one would guess, the part of the book in which many inquiring readers find themselves being caught up by the spell Lewis was weaving.[16] Using clarifying analogies, Lewis provided a lucid summary of the essential teachings that Christians over the centuries have agreed on, no easy task in itself. At the same time he confronted his audience with engaging arguments as to why the classic Christian accounts of reality and human experience are more compelling than any of the alternatives. Without watering down Christianity to meet modern tastes, he summarized basic teachings that might often be dismissed as far-fetched and explained why he, as a former unbeliever, had found them to in fact make far better sense than any other view.

Lewis's most famous and also most debated argument in that respect is that it would be foolish to claim, as liberal Christians and others do, that Jesus was a great moral teacher but not God. Lewis's argument, adapted from earlier apologists, is that if Jesus's claim to be God was false, he was either a liar as evil as

CHAPTER TWO

the Devil in Hell, or he was a lunatic on a par with "the man who says he is a poached egg." "You must make your choice."[17] Throughout these broadcasts, Lewis attempted to turn the tables on much of the standard thinking of the day about religion. Classic Christianity, which one might have thought was outdated and on the defensive, emerged in Lewis's telling as the only sensible alternative left standing.

At the end of the fifth and final broadcast of this series, Lewis offered a virtual altar call. Having presented by way of analogy that the incarnation is like an "invasion" in which God has landed behind the lines in a world occupied by the enemy, or the powers of evil, he explained that God is delaying pushing on to the inevitable end-time victory so that we might have a chance to *freely* choose the right side before the battle is over. "Now, today, this moment, is our chance to choose the right side," he concluded. "God is holding back to give us that chance. It will not last for ever. We must take it or leave it."[18]

Within a week of the last of these broadcasts, Fenn responded with thanks and more praise ("I don't think they could have been improved") and asked if Lewis would do a third series for the Forces Network broadcast in the fall.[19] Lewis accepted but put off the preparation to the summer. These would be eight talks on ethical topics. He wrote that he had considered as an overall title: "Christian Morals, Christian Morality, and Christian Moral Standards." But he settled on "Christian Behaviour." "All the other words have been more or less spoiled. I think that if Aristotle were writing now he'd call the Ethics, 'Behaviour.'"[20]

By the time Lewis got and accepted this invitation, in February 1942, the United States had been drawn into the war, and the Axis attack on the Soviet Union the previous spring had made any invasion of England unlikely. Yet even without blitz bombing, the times were not at all bright. Much of the British public thought that the United States was getting what it deserved for trying to sit out the war. During the early months of 1942 the Allies continued to be pushed back on fronts all over the world, and there was increasing unrest at home.[21]

Lewis, as someone who was now to lecture the nation on morality, had his own often turbulent home front as a training ground. During the years of these broadcasts, he was dealing with a steadily declining domestic situation as the health of Mrs. Moore, now in her seventies, deteriorated. Late in 1941 he wrote to Sister Penelope, "Pray for Jane. . . . She is the old lady I call my mother and live with (she is really the mother of a friend)—an unbeliever, ill, old, frightened, full of charity in the sense of alms, but full of uncharity in several other senses. And I can do so little for her."[22] Mrs. Moore, or Minto, suffered from painful varicose ulcers that seemed to bring out her quarrelsome and irascible side. Jack was by all accounts dedicated to serving her. Warnie Lewis, who, for mysterious reasons probably related to his alcoholism, was discharged from regular army service in mid-1940 and returned home, had an especially dim view of her. In his diary Warnie lamented the degree to which, in his view, Jack was enslaved to her. Minto's charitable side was manifested in opening their home to refugee children since the outset of the war. As he wrote to Dorothy Sayers early in 1942, Jack found these, on the whole, to be "delightful creatures."[23] These evacuee girls came and went but could be a great aid in the often dysfunctional household. Particularly helpful was Jill Flewett, who was sixteen when she arrived in 1943 and stayed for nearly two years, helping to keep the household in order. Jill acknowledges having had an immense crush on Jack and seems to have been adored by everyone. She recalled that Jack's relation to Minto "was unlike any other mother–son relationship I had ever seen. It was so devoted. He was so caring and wonderful with her, and she doted on him."[24]

Having taken on the role of a Christian apologist, Lewis seems to have sensed the problems involved in trying to make one's private life conform to one's public testimony. Already in October 1940, at the time he was writing *The Screwtape Letters*, he had adopted the practice of making a weekly confession to an Anglican confessor. "The decision to do so," he reported to Sister Penelope, "was one of the hardest I have ever made, but now I am committed." He later reported that he had gotten cold feet and tried to fish the letter out of the mailbox.[25] Nonetheless, the discipline must have bolstered him in taking on the task of lecturing the nation on "Christian Behaviour."

Lewis, who was never good with numbers, seemed not to have noticed that this third set of broadcasts, which Fenn had said would be on the Forces Network from 2:50 to 3:00 Sunday afternoons, would be five minutes shorter than his earlier broadcasts. When he sent his manuscripts to the BBC to be typed, they discovered the discrepancy. So each of the texts had to be cut by a third to fit the ten-minute broadcasts.[26] Lewis delivered these eight brief talks from September to November 1942.

These presentations he titled "Christian Behaviour" contrasted with the rest of what became *Mere Christianity* in that they dealt less often with grand cosmic matters regarding the Christian account of reality. Instead, Lewis explained and defended everyday Christian moral principles, though always keeping the cosmic context in view. Whatever Lewis's reasons for choosing these more practical subjects for his series of Sunday-afternoon addresses for the Forces Network, he was not planning that a decade later it would become the third part of a larger book on basic Christian teaching. Yet even if the future book 3 of *Mere Christianity* turned out to be, like a third movement in a symphony, a change of pace, it fit with the whole. It also made good sense as a sequel to the first two parts in that, building on the earlier presentations of the sometimes startling claims of undiluted Christianity, it related these to much more practical everyday questions of how Christians ought to live.

Lewis used musical analogies in describing "the three parts of morality" as fair play or harmony among individuals, harmonizing *within* each individual, and pursuing the purpose of human life, or playing the "tune the conductor of the band wants it to play."[27] In the subsequent broadcasts he took on the topics of social morality, psychoanalysis and morality, sexual morality, forgiveness, "the great sin" of pride, and Christian faith, to which he devoted two presentations.

As could be expected, Lewis's broadcast called "Sexual Morality" drew the most immediate attention. Somehow a tabloid, *The Daily Mirror*, got the script and without authorization published it under the title "This Was a Very Frank Talk Which We Think Everyone Should Read." In fact, Lewis had not said anything particularly frank. He had said that the modern world cheapens sex. Christianity, he observed, is almost the only major religion that thoroughly approves of the body, but it does include the unpopular teaching of chastity outside of marriage. Such chastity requires often-renewed dependence on God. Perhaps the tabloid liked it that he said that, contrary to popular views, sexual sins are not the worst sort. "The sins of the flesh are bad, but are the least bad of all sins."[28] Hearing of the pirating from Fenn, Lewis shot back (his entire letter was on a strip of paper an inch and a half high), "Thanks for letting me know about 'The Daily Mirror'—damn their impudence."[29] Appropriately, the succeeding broadcast dealt with "Forgiveness."

Soon after completing the series, Lewis revised it for publication as a second little paperback, *Christian Behaviour*, which would appear in April 1943. For this published version he restored whatever had been cut from the broadcasts. He also added four additional chapters, "The Cardinal Virtues," "Christian Marriage," "Charity," and "Hope."[30] The addition of major reference to cultivating traditional virtues (the four "Cardinal" virtues, prudence, temperance, justice, and fortitude, which "all civilized people recognize," and the three "Theological" virtues, faith, hope, and charity) grounded the presentations deeply in a core Christian tradition. Practicing virtues, Lewis explained, is like becoming a good tennis player rather than occasionally making a good shot.[31] In contrast, adding a chapter called "Christian Marriage" got him into a topic on which, by his own admission, he had no expertise. Eventually, as we shall see, that chapter became one of the most contested, not so much for his views of marriage itself as for his conventional mid-twentieth-century views of gender roles.

During the course of 1942 Lewis was becoming, rather suddenly, a celebrity. He was already well known for the wireless talks. As an early review of "Christian Behaviour" put it, he was "a born broadcaster,"[32] and the BBC was very pleased by the reception of his talks. Even so, it was hardly the case that, as is sometimes claimed, his was one of the very best-known voices in England. Lewis's broadcasts each typically drew between 1 and 1.5 million listeners. As Bruce L. Johnson points out, his broadcast "Sexual Morality," on October 11, 1942, drew 1.5 million listeners, whereas, by comparison, the BBC news that evening drew 16 million.[33] Further, as Stephanie Derrick documents in her study of the context of Lewis's broadcasts, quite a few other BBC religious broadcasters were, like Lewis, explaining basics of Christianity to laypeople. Several of these also published their presentations, often with the subtitle "Broadcast Talks." For instance, the Reverend Ronald Selby Wright, a BBC regular known as "The Radio Padre," who had a much larger following on the air than did Lewis, published *The Average Man: Broadcast Talk*, in 1942.[34] Lewis's occasional sets of ten- or fifteen-minute broadcasts plus a few other appearances on religious talk shows would have by themselves made him well known, but not quite famous.

More significant, certainly in his own eyes, in suddenly making Lewis into a minor celebrity was the remarkable success of *The Screwtape Letters*. These came out as a book in February 1942 in a modest print run of two thousand that sold out immediately. The demand was so great that Lewis's publisher, Geoffrey Bles, reprinted it twice in March and six more times by the end of the year. Macmillan, a major New York publisher, offered an American edition in 1943 that similarly became a great hit.[35] These publishing triumphs helped ensure attention on both sides of the Atlantic for the little paperback editions of the radio addresses. Bles published *Broadcast Talks* in July 1942, and Macmillan offered that the next year with the catchier title *The Case for*

*Christianity.* Especially in America, where Lewis had been virtually unknown, the fact that this slim book and its sequels of the next two years, *Christian Behavior* and *Beyond Personality*, were by the author of *Screwtape* helped guarantee that they would be noticed.

Lewis was enjoying his celebrity. In January 1943 he wrote to Arthur Greeves, "You will have noticed that I have been having great luck with my books lately, and it wd. be affectation to pretend I hadn't gotten much pleasure out of it: but the catch is that it increases the amount of letters one has to write almost beyond endurance."[36] One of the immediate benefits of fame was that it opened doors for him to other celebrities. Lewis was particularly pleased to hear early in 1942 from Dorothy Sayers, who complimented him on *The Screwtape Letters*. Lewis and Sayers had much in common. They were both lay Anglicans and fiction writers. Sayers, like Lewis, had recently turned to presenting popular reflections on traditional Christianity, notably in her *Mind of the Maker* in 1941. Sayers wanted Lewis to contribute to a series of such books she was editing, but he was in the midst of so many projects that he declined. James Welch and Eric Fenn had also recruited Sayers for what became a series of very controversial but also highly successful BBC broadcasts of her radio play on the life of Jesus, "The Man Born to Be King," which was presented in twelve broadcasts during 1941 and 1942. Soon after Sayers wrote to Lewis, the two met in Oxford. They became valued correspondents to one another.

By now Lewis was so clearly a success that the BBC wanted to enlist him as often as possible. He and Eric Fenn had already talked of a fourth set of talks, this time on more theological subjects. But Lewis wanted these postponed. Apparently he had expressed some concerns about resentments among his Oxford colleagues regarding taking time away for such non-academic work.[37] Also, Lewis was tremendously busy. The war had greatly reduced the number of students he had to tutor, but in addition to RAF lecturing, he had been writing at a furious rate. In December 1941 he delivered at University College in North Wales a series of lectures that he expanded and published late in 1942 as *A Preface to Paradise Lost*. By the spring of 1942 he had also finished the second of his interplanetary novels, *Perelandra*, published in April 1943. In February 1943 he delivered a set of lectures at the University of Durham in which he leveled a scathing critique of how modern philosophies were undermining the moral dimensions of general education. In the lectures and the resulting book, *The Abolition of Man*, published later in 1943, he elaborated on a point made in his first set of broadcasts, that there were some basic moral principles, what Lewis called the "Tao," common to all cultures. For relaxation Lewis was still meeting with the Inklings and reading their works. During this period he was the principal reader and midwife for what became Tolkien's *Lord of the Rings*.[38]

Eric Fenn waited until March, after Lewis had finished his "Abolition of Man" lectures, to follow up regarding a fourth set of talks later that year. Fenn now suggested a series for the Forces Network in July and August, again on Sunday afternoons, to be called "Misconceptions of Christianity." Lewis said he was too busy for 1943 but might do a series at a later date. Fenn came back with a suggestion that, in the meantime, Lewis might contribute a single broadcast to a Home Service series called "Why I Believe in God." Lewis responded: "Not my pigeon, I think. . . . Not that personal 'testifying' isn't most important, but it isn't my gift."[39]

Not to be deterred, the BBC turned up the pressure by having James Welch himself write to Lewis to ask him to appear on a discussion show about religion called *The Anvil*. Uncharacteristically, Lewis accepted this as a one-time proposition in July.[40]

Soon Eric Fenn was also back, now with a topic that was clearly within Lewis's range of interests. Would Lewis do a talk on *Paradise Lost*?[41] Lewis responded on a strip of paper just two inches high to say that such a talk would be "an absolute waste of time. What's the good of telling them they'll enjoy it, when we both know they won't?"[42]

Fenn returned to the topic of the theological talks. He also asked if Lewis knew anyone to do a monthly review of religious books, or if even Lewis himself would care to. Lewis declined the book review job, but now he was ready with a sketch of seven talks on theological topics. These would include two on the Trinity and one each on the Creation, the Incarnation, the two natures of Christ, the Resurrection, and the Ascension.[43]

Most of Lewis's notes to the BBC were written or typed on tiny scraps of paper. Fenn finally commented, "If I may say so, your passion for paper economy exceeds anything my imagination can grasp!" Lewis soon responded in a brief note confirming some arrangements for the *Anvil* program, but using a full sheet of paper and leaving a wide unused margin. "And what about paper economy now?" he quipped. "I trust I can do a handsome thing when put on my mettle. P. S. You may use the margin of this letter for any purpose you like."[44]

The talks on theological topics would be for the Home Service and would not be presented until the next winter, but in the meantime they ran into more complications than any of the others. First, Lewis delayed submitting the scripts until December because he could not find a suitable typist. So as not to risk losing the sole pen-and-ink manuscripts in the mail, he had them delivered to the BBC by hand. But when they were typed, Fenn noticed that this time they were too short. Once again Lewis had missed a mathematical detail, though now in the opposite direction to that of his earlier error. He had written for ten-, not fifteen-minute, broadcasts. Fenn gave Lewis the option of giving up the extra five minutes, but Lewis chose the more complex task of adding about six hundred words to each of the seven scripts. The necessity of this revision also brought lengthy editorial suggestions from Fenn, though Lewis did not seem to alter the content in any substantial way. Lewis also kept his title "Beyond Personality," despite some urging for something that would more clearly reveal his subject. The full title would be "Beyond Personality—the Christian Idea of God." Then came the real blow. On February 8 Fenn wrote to Lewis to explain that, because of changes in the Forces Programme, the Home Service broadcasts had to be drastically rearranged and Lewis's talks had to be scheduled for 10:20 p.m., with the first to be given on February 22, 1944. Fenn said he had tried every alternative and suggested that the broadcasts might be recorded—even though audiences responded less well to talks that were announced as being recorded.[45]

Lewis was incensed by this late change of plans. "Pox on your 'powers'!" he shot back. "Who the devil is going to listen at 10:20?" His first suggestion was to postpone the whole thing, but he realized it must be too late for that. Because he could not stay in London on Tuesday evenings, broadcasting at 10:20 would mean catching a late train and getting back to Oxford at 3 a.m. Still, Lewis relented from his understandable fury enough to compromise and say, "Well, I'll give *three* under those conditions." The rest he would record on the evenings he came in. He then managed to turn his anger into humor:

> If you know the address of any reliable firm of assassins, nose-slitters, garrotters and poisoners I should be grateful to have it.

I shall write a book about the BBC—you see if I don't! Gr-r-r-r!!⁴⁶

Lewis began this late-night final series of broadcasts by observing that "everyone has warned me" that "'the ordinary listener' doesn't want Theology; you give him plain practical religion." He complimented his audience by saying they were not children and that his experience, as in talking to the RAF, was that laypeople are often deeply interested in doctrine. He went on, in one of his most helpful images, to explain that theology is like a good map when one is going on a journey and so is very practical.⁴⁷ He proceeded with his characteristic use of analogies to the daunting task of explaining the Christian doctrines of the Trinity and the Incarnation. He presented these, with his usual assurance, not as obstacles to Christian belief but rather as unique qualities of Christianity that enhance its attractiveness. He went on through the series of broadcasts leading listeners through more analogies to see the intensely practical and challenging implications for themselves.

Only one of Lewis's talks was broadcast in the United States. In March of 1944, NBC presented the next-to-last talk of the series, "Is Christianity Hard or Easy?" That was appropriate as a stand-alone talk because it got to the heart of both the challenge and the promise of grace toward which Lewis was leading his listeners. In this talk he explained how Jesus can say not only "Take up your cross" but also "My yoke is easy and my burden is light." Here he used the analogy that we humans are like eggs that need to be hatched if we ever are to fly, something that happens to us but also something that we have to do. We are meant to be united to Christ. "This is the whole of Christianity," he said with startling simplicity. "The Church exists for nothing else but to draw men into Christ, to make them little Christs."[48]

This series of talks also gives us glimpses of some differences in organization between the original talks and the subsequent book version. Soon after the broadcasts, Lewis added four new chapters and made some other changes for the publication of the third book of broadcasts, *Beyond Personality—The Christian Idea of God*, which appeared in England in October 1944. The most striking illustration of the changes can be found by listening to the last broadcast from the series, which is the only surviving recording (readily found on YouTube). Lewis started by filling in the first five minutes with a response to some listeners' questions regarding how God can hear all our prayers at once. This material now appears as the beginning of chapter 3 of the book. In the broadcast he turned from this digression to his original ten-minute script of "The New Man." Here he argued that Christians who give up preoccupation with self and are united to Christ represent, in a sense, a new step in the evolution of humanity. He concluded with a direct evangelistic appeal: "Look for Christ and you'll get Him, and with Him, everything else thrown in. Look for yourself and you'll get only hatred, loneliness, despair, and ruin." He slowed down as he spoke these last words in a doleful cadence for his last-night audience. In the book versions he reverses these concluding sentences (though adding "rage" and "decay" to the warnings) and ends on the upbeat promise of the new life in Christ.[49]

For this last series of talks Lewis finally got his wish that they be immediately published in the BBC newspaper, *The Listener*.[50] That provided a forum for some strong reactions in the letters column. Predictably, a number of readers were upset simply by Lewis's advocacy of such a traditional form of Christianity.[51] The BBC also conducted surveys of their listeners. One thing they found was that the late-night time slot took a larger toll on week-to-week listeners than might have been hoped.[52] Eric Fenn reported, moreover, on the basis of responses to Lewis's second broadcast ("The Three-Personal God"), that the audience was sharply divided. "They obviously either regard you as 'the cat's whiskers' or as 'beneath contempt.'"[53]

# Loved or Hated

Lewis was hardly surprised to learn that listeners' responses to his broadcasts were so sharply divided. The letters he received, he reported, were "nearly all either violent abuse or extravagant praise."[1] But he did not view the reactions as so much about himself. "The two views you report (Cat's whiskers and Beneath Contempt)," he responded to Fenn, "aren't very illuminating about *me* perhaps: about my subject matter, it is an old story, isn't it. They love, or hate."[2] As a university don who had committed the unpardonable academic sin of becoming a radio evangelist, Lewis already had to have had a thick skin in order to deal with the witty, condescending scorn of many of his colleagues.

His broadcasts aroused some similarly predictable reactions among anti-Christian elements in the public press. Eric Fenn remarked in 1942 that Lewis might take "particular satisfaction" that his talks had "risen to the level of a *cause celebre* in the columns of the 'Free Thinker.'"[3] The *Freethinker*, a weekly notorious for its atheism, kept up a barrage of attacks on Lewis and the BBC. The editor, Chapmen Cohen, was especially indignant that the BBC should give a Christian a pulpit "where no one shall be permitted to criticize him from that platform." Cohen insisted that Lewis and other Christian apologists simply ignored "what we *know* to be the origin of the belief in gods." Seventy years of scientific research, readily found in books such as Sir James George Frazer's famous turn-of-the-century work *The Golden Bough*, demonstrated "the origin of the gods in the ignorance and weakness of primitive humanity. Substantially this is now the scientific position," Cohen declared.[4]

George Orwell, writing in 1944 in his column for the left-wing newspaper *Tribune*, lamented Lewis's "vogue at this moment" and "the exaggerated praise he has received" and was similarly dismissive. Reviewing *Beyond Personality*, Orwell ridiculed its chummy tone and "Edwardian slang like 'awfully,' 'jolly well,' . . . and so forth." It was, said Orwell, just another "silly-clever religious book" of the type that had been "endemic in England for quite sixty years." All of these claim that the objections to Christianity are merely old hat. They also seem to easily demolish writers "associated in the popular mind with Science and Rationalism," such as T. H. Huxley, H. G. Wells, or Bertrand Russell, though Orwell added, "I notice that most of the demolished ones are still there, while some of the Christian apologists begin to look rather faded." Orwell also thought talks such as Lewis's were "not really so unpolitical as they are meant to look" but rather part of a concerted "out-flanking movement" against the left.[5]

By way of contrast, most of the mainstream British press in this era, perhaps especially during the war, tended to provide respectful views regarding Christianity. So, for instance, the prestigious *Times Literary Supplement* (*TLS*) offered one of the earliest reviews of *Broadcast Talks* in a wholly laudatory short notice published in September 1942. The reviewer described Lewis's account of *What Christians Believe* as "a lucid exposition" in which "the author shows how neither atheism, pantheism, nor dualism can offer a comparable solution to the questions that await man's answer about the universe, about God, and (more particularly) about the Devil."[6]

When the third paperback, *Beyond Personality*, appeared in 1944, *TLS* gave it a fuller review that could almost be described as bubbling with enthusiasm. "Mr. Lewis has a quite unique power of making theology an attractive, exciting and (one might almost say) an uproariously fascinating quest." The reviewer was impressed that Lewis had been able to keep radio audiences listening to expositions of theological topics such as the Incarnation or the Trinity. "But Mr. Lewis fascinates us by his boyish pleasure in presenting to us what most people regard as a dismal and purely abstract science." As a convert, "he cannot help shouting for joy over his discovery." Lewis, the wholly friendly reviewer observed, "rather than condescending to his listeners and readers, tells them they are neither infants nor

CHAPTER THREE

nit-wits, and helps them to share in his own '*excitement*' in reflecting on these profound themes."[7]

Reviews in religious periodicals were, predictably, more mixed, reflecting the spectrum of Christian outlooks. Roman Catholic publications were at first largely enthusiastic about Lewis's work and welcomed his defense of broadly Christian orthodoxy. At the same time, one careful Catholic analysis of *Beyond Personality*, while mostly applauding Lewis, pointed out that his doctrine of salvation was not the Catholic view. "The attainment of sonship appears here," cautioned G. D. Smith, the editor of the *Clergy Review*, "not as an instantaneous transformation of the soul sacramentally produced, but as a laborious process by which a man gradually changes his behavior." In correcting Lewis, Smith said that he was doing so only because of "the very influence which the author exerts upon Christian thought in this country which seems to make it worth while to indicate the one conception—and that an essential conception which his theology needs in order to bring it into line with Catholic teaching."[8]

In British Protestant circles the reception was sharply divided along the fault line between more traditional Christians and those who were modernists, or liberals, theologically. On the more traditionalist side was much unbridled enthusiasm. Often that came from mainstream clergy, who, like many ordinary churchgoers, were thrilled to have orthodoxy so winningly presented. *The Screwtape Letters*, combined with Lewis's being a regular on the wireless, had turned him into a minor sensation among proponents of more traditional Christianity. Following in the wake of *Screwtape*, the inexpensive paperbacks of the broadcast talks soon became comparably popular. *Christian Behaviour*, for instance, which was released in England in April 1943, had already sold about sixty thousand copies by the end of November that same year.[9] As one disgruntled critic summarized the phenomenon shortly after the end of the war, "The writings of Mr. C. S. Lewis have been received with such a degree of acclamation almost unique in our time, distinguished periodicals vying with religious papers . . . in praising his wit, profundity, force, originality, and brilliance."[10]

Progressive Protestants were alarmed that the popularity of Lewis's backward-looking Christianity was undoing centuries of theological progress. In 1944 E. George Lee, a Unitarian, in a thirty-two-page pamphlet titled "C. S. Lewis and Some Modern Theologians," argued that the war had brought a failure of theological nerve among most Anglican churchmen so that they had become reluctant to speak out on the basis of what they knew to be a growing consensus of modern scholarship. Such scholarship rendered obsolete any claims for exclusive Christian truth based on the unique authority of biblical revelation. Yet the "general reactionary tendency" of the times had brought to life what Lee described as "B. B. C. Christianity." In order to reassure people, proponents of old-fashioned views committed "treachery of the intellect in order to try to find repose in the emotions." C. S.

CHAPTER THREE

Lewis had proved to be the worst offender in reasserting orthodoxy and arguing, for instance, for the divinity of Christ while ignoring the proven unreliability of the Gospels.[11]

In 1945 the *Modern Churchman*, a journal dedicated to modernist Christianity, published a careful and scathing attack, "The Theology of C. S. Lewis." The author, E. L. Allen, a theological scholar who had written on Kierkegaard, noted with chagrin that in a local bookshop there were a dozen or more copies available of Lewis's books from the broadcast talks. He likewise reported that a friend, without having read the books himself, had ordered a number of these to give to lay preachers simply on the basis of Lewis's reputation. Allen believed that Lewis was preaching mainly to the already converted and "playing to the gallery" while neglecting the serious honest seekers who were "dissatisfied with traditional presentations of Christianity." Lewis represented his as simply the "'central tradition'" of Christianity, but it was really based on the Pauline writings versus the Jesus of the Gospels. It was also "Augustinian" and a throwback to "the Middle Ages in its most superstitious phases." Lewis offered an authoritarian gospel that "in a world smitten with the rival madnesses of Fascism and Marxism" fell into "the temptation to oppose dogmatism with dogmatism rather than with freedom." Lewis combined a "'Take it or leave it'" attitude with "*crudity*" of thought. Particularly his arguments regarding the divinity of Jesus ignored generations of biblical scholarship that offered compelling alternative interpretations. On "any other book than the New Testament, Mr. Lewis would have taken pains to acquaint himself with recent work on the subject."[12]

The next year the *Modern Churchman* followed this theological critique with one equally cutting from R. C. Churchill, a literary scholar. Churchill first argued at length against the majority of reviewers, who predicted that *The Screwtape Letters* would become "'a great religious classic.'" He was especially offended that Lewis could get away with dismissing so many of the major trends in modern thought with a sneer rather than an argument. Even if talking about devils in *Screwtape* were excused as a literary device, Churchill found it "preposterous" that in *Broadcast Talks* Lewis argued for the reality of Satan in modern times. Lewis, said Churchill, claimed in *Beyond Personality* that he was not treating his audience as children. But the opposite was the case. Lewis used rhetoric in place of mature reason. If Lewis's arguments for the reality of the Devil were an example of something worthy not only of the simple layperson but also of "the mature philosopher," as one church periodical had claimed, "then I'd sooner have the 'Christianity-and-water' which Mr. Lewis pokes so much fun at; I think personally, it's preferable to Christianity-and-ginger-beer." As to the argument that Jesus was either a fraud, a madman, or who he said he was, Churchill maintained, as did the other critics, that mature modern thought and biblical scholarship showed that

Jesus was not divine. Nonetheless, Jesus was a great moral teacher and the modern world still needed his guidance, along with that of other great teachers such as Plato, Aristotle, and Confucius. By disparaging the idea that if we just listened to Jesus we might have a better moral order, "Mr. Lewis's three series of radio talks have done a grave disservice to European civilization."[13]

Though widely popular, Lewis remained a highly divisive figure in Great Britain, in part just because of his popularity. Having been a radio broadcaster made him a public figure about whom people were likely to form a strong opinion. Dorothy Sayers captured how controversial he still was when she wrote to a friend in 1948: "Do you like C. S. Lewis' work, or are you one of the people who foam at the mouth when they hear his name?"[14]

Lewis's reception in wartime America was, on the whole, even more enthusiastic than in England and less mixed with sharp criticism. Prior to 1943 Lewis was hardly known in the United States.[15] Nonetheless, when Macmillan issued the American edition of *The Screwtape Letters* in February 1943, Lewis's American reputation catapulted from obscure to prominent. By early July 1943, the *New York Times* was noting that *Screwtape* had gone into its sixth printing and that Macmillan's fall list would include *The Problem of Pain*, *Out of the Silent Planet*, and *The Case for Christianity* (the American title for *Broadcast Talks*).[16] *Christian*

*Behaviour* would follow by January 1944 and *Beyond Personality* in March 1945.

The mainstream American press first lauded Lewis for *The Screwtape Letters*. In March 1943 the *New York Times* reviewer noted that the book was already celebrated among "the well-bombed British" and was deserving of its reputation even if "what the New World will think of it remains to be seen."[17] In April America's leading news magazine, *Time*, proclaimed, "The sharpest religo-psychological writer of the season is an elderly devil named Screwtape, whose letters of instruction have somehow fallen into the hands of C. S. Lewis, Fellow of Oxford's Magdalen College."[18] The same month the influential *Saturday Review* offered a rave from the poet and critic Leonard Bacon. He disclaimed having "the talents to analyze the most exciting piece of Christian apologetics that has turned up in a long time." Bacon believed it was only a slight stretch when some English enthusiasts compared Lewis to Jonathan Swift and thought that "believer and unbeliever alike may give thanks" for "a spectacular and satisfactory nova in the bleak sky of satire."[19] Edward A. Golden of Monogram Pictures obtained a six-months' option on the motion picture rights, but the Lewises turned down the project.[20]

The triumph of *Screwtape* brought in its wake attention to the other books, including the little one-dollar paperback of the radio talks. In January 1944 *Time* published a review of *Christian Behaviour*. Noting that by then Americans and Britons had bought some two hundred thousand copies of *Screwtape*, *Time* observed that Dante and Milton had found it easier to write about Hell than about Heaven but that in *Christian Behaviour* "Lewis succeeded in the much tougher task of making Heaven as readable as Hell." *Time* went on to provide a brief character sketch of Lewis, including that he lived in a rambling house "with his foster mother and brother" and that he "likes to sit up late at night in college rooms talking nonsense, poetry, theology, metaphysics over beer, tea and pipes." And it offered the first published instance of what became a well-known Lewis remark, "There's no sound I like better than adult male laughter."[21]

By the spring of 1944, as Americans were waiting for D-Day, Lewis's stock in the mainstream media went a notch higher as he was featured on the cover of the *Saturday Review*. Leonard Bacon provided another rave, this time about Lewis's new interplanetary novel, *Perelandra*: "Mr. Lewis is beyond question one of the most exciting and satisfactory writers who has come to the surface of the maelstrom of these turbulent times." Even though Bacon confessed to being unable to share Lewis's orthodoxy, he admired that the Oxford don had "clearly got himself born for the second time" and that his "convictions are so genuine and so vigorously, if courteously, defended that it may properly be said that one is often most interested when least in agreement with his premises."[22]

Around the same time the *New York Times Book Review* (*NYTBR*) provided an enthusiastic review of

*Christian Behaviour.* "Every now and then in the English universities," wrote Henry James Forman, "there arises some don or teacher who is so clear-headed and expresses himself so well that . . . all of England is eager to listen to him." Even though "the British Broadcasting Company may and does show a scarcity of commercials about soap and chewing gum," it excelled in featuring such a speaker and thinker as Lewis to speak on a wide range of Christian topics with such clarity.[23] The next year the *Times* provided another glowing review, this time of *Beyond Personality.* The reviewer, P. W. Wilson, observed that Lewis "continues to be the major apostle of Christian faith for the man in the street." Wilson cautioned that Lewis was an evangelist out literally for our souls: "He is unsatisfied that we should be 'nice people.' He requires that we be 'new men,' and no revivalist has ever set forth 'life changing' in terms more challenging to the individual." Even though some might say Lewis was simplifying in his presentation of this old Gospel message, Wilson maintained that his "scintillating volume" dealt with matters too profound and mysterious not to be taken seriously.[24]

There was one major exception to this adulation in the mainstream American press, and this devil's advocate had, like Screwtape himself, British origins. In April 1944 the *New Republic* published a blistering denunciation of Lewis by an impressive young English-born journalist and broadcaster named Alistair Cooke. Cooke had immigrated to America and become an

American citizen in 1941. He later became famous as the urbane host of *Masterpiece Theater* and for his *Letter from America* broadcasts that ran on BBC world services for over half a century. His father had been a lay Methodist minister, and the son preached with the fervor of a convert rescued from the constraints of evangelicalism. "We may wonder at the alarming vogue of Mr. C. S. Lewis," he wrote, "whose harmless fantasies about the kingdom of God and Evil . . . have had modest literary success, while multitude of readers, and in Britain radio listeners, succumb to the charm of his more direct treatises on Christian conduct." The "personal insecurity" of the war, Cooke believed, quite evidently explained such reactionary phenomena. Not only do wars "spawn so many quack religions and Messiahs," but they also thrust figures like Lewis "into the limelight, for in doubting times completely unremarkable minor prophets are pressed into making a career of reassurance."[25]

Cooke was especially alarmed at the potential influence of *Christian Behaviour*. In ordinary times, the printed broadcasts would have come and gone harmlessly with only polite notice. But, he wrote, "from the way they were received in Britain, and from the eagerness of American networks to have Mr. Lewis shed light on our own dark continent, it may be assumed that the personal values of several million Britons and Americans stand in imminent danger of the befuddlement at which Mr. Lewis is so transparently adroit." Cooke acknowledged that "Mr. Lewis has a real radio talent," thus making his views especially dangerous.[26]

Cooke objected most passionately to Lewis's conventional views of sexual morality. Lewis's assertion "that extra-marital sex is monstrous because 'it isolates one kind of union from all the other kinds of union which were intended to go along with it'" brought from Cooke the parenthetical response "(by the same reasoning, it must be equally irresponsible to lunch with friends you don't live with)." Cooke offered few arguments against Lewis but rather disparaged his views. He suggested that Lewis, as a bachelor, had fears about talking about sexual morality. Cooke also derided *Perelandra* (in whose Eden naked people had not yet discovered sex) as "embarrassing" and "the natural and arid, counterpart of "Christian Behaviour.'" He even ridiculed Lewis for using italics for emphasis (Lewis removed these from *Mere Christianity*).[27]

Although Cooke's denunciation in the *New Republic* was the conspicuous exception to the rule in the American public press, which seems to have had almost nothing but adulation for Lewis,[28] in religious journals, as in England, American commentators were more likely to qualify their praise with a few doctrinal reservations. The Jesuit magazine *America* provided an early enthusiastic notice for *The Case for Christianity*, as did *Catholic World*, in which the reviewer observed, "If this is not the book that a Catholic would have written, it says very many things that desperately need to be said. Armies of men are groping their way back to the religion of Christ; this book will facilitate greatly that sacred journey."[29] In *Commonweal* Anne Fremantle, a British convert to Catholicism, praised Lewis's *Beyond Personality* and noted the resentments from the left and the unorthodox that the BBC gave airtime only to the orthodox and had made Lewis preeminent among its religious "radio stars." But she also found Lewis to have "a very picayune view of the Church" and wondered "just how many of 'those who profess and call themselves Christian,' rather than Catholic, would agree with anything Mr. Lewis says." *America* printed a rave review of *Beyond Personality* in May of 1945, but then an irate letter from one influential clerical critic, citing the British Catholic criticism of Lewis, forced the reviewer to publish a partial retraction.[30]

That incident was followed by a more serious condemnation of *Beyond Personality* by Malachi J. Donnelly, SJ, in the *American Ecclesiastical Review*. Donnelly, too, cited as conclusive the Very Reverend G. D. Smith's arguments in the British *Clergy Review* that Lewis contradicted Catholic doctrine. Moreover, he pointed out that Catholics were forbidden, according to canon law, from reading a book on theology unless it was "morally certain" that the "book contains nothing contrary to the Catholic faith." Otherwise they must "obtain the required permission from the proper ecclesiastical authority." Yet, Donnelly lamented, almost all the Catholic reviewers to date had recommended the book, even though *Beyond Personality* "teaches and is largely founded on a false doctrine of the supernatural life; it is tainted with modernistic tendencies with regard to divine Revelation and the Church; and finally, it has a distinct inclination (in some respects) toward religious indifferentism." Donnelly urged that in the future reviewers in Catholic periodicals should observe the clear law of the Church.[31]

Mainline American Protestants (meaning those affiliated with the major denominations, such as Methodist, (northern) Baptist, (northern) Presbyterian, Congregationalist, Episcopalian, Lutheran, Disciples, and others) were much less likely than Catholics to question Lewis's orthodoxy. Most clergy and laity in such denominations were traditionalist enough to appreciate Lewis but also broad-minded enough to not worry about fine points of doctrine. Whatever criticisms there might be were likely to come from those on the theological left, who would find Lewis too orthodox. Unquestionably, the leading American voice of modernist and liberal Christianity was the *Christian Century*, edited by the venerable Charles Clayton Morrison. Unlike the *Modern Churchman* in England, during the war years the *Christian Century* did not publish polemics regarding Lewis. Rather, it gave him only passing attention, publishing a few short notices of his books, typically offering some praise but also reservations, such as that he was sometimes too chatty and superficial.[32] Some other mainline voices were more enthusiastic. For instance, the influential clergyman and editor of the *Christian Herald*, Daniel A. Poling, offered an early recommendation of *The Case for*

*Christianity*.[33] And a reviewer in the *Anglican Theological Journal* wrote of *Christian Behaviour* that "certainly every Churchman should possess this book," and "our confirmation classes ought to have more teaching of this sort."[34]

*Theology Today*, the respected theological journal published by Princeton Theological Seminary, offered nothing but praise in a lengthy review of Lewis's works published early in 1945. The reviewer, Edward D. Myers of Trinity College, Connecticut, wrote of *The Case for Christianity* and *Christian Behaviour* that Lewis gives "not only the Christian interpretation of moral problems but also a fresh interpretation of Christianity." Myers noted that interpreters of all sorts had appreciated that "his account is Christian and not sectarian in the sense that it is peculiarly Episcopal or Roman Catholic or Presbyterian or Methodist" and said, "That his efforts are largely successful is acclaimed by all the critics." He added in a footnote that Alistair Cooke was the one exception.[35]

Late in 1946, the *Christian Century* joined in recognizing that Lewis was becoming a star in the American religious resurgence of the era by publishing a laudatory account of an interview with Lewis. The Reverend George C. Anderson, rector of the Episcopal church in Swarthmore, Pennsylvania (a church that another British convert, W. H Auden attended), had visited Lewis in his rooms at Magdalen College. Anderson began by exaggerating Lewis's fame as a broadcaster on the BBC, claiming that his voice was almost as familiar to British listeners as was the sound of Big Ben striking each hour. Anderson reported conversations regarding various prominent thinkers and topics, such as Kierkegaard, Reinhold Niebuhr, Karl Barth, and existentialism, none of which Lewis professed to understand very well. Nonetheless, Anderson believed that even though Lewis was a layman, he was one of the twentieth century's most effective opponents of humanism, by which he meant human-centered philosophies. "Lewis," he reported, "feels that current humanistic teaching is anti-Christian and that men who accept this philosophy should not be in the Christian church." Even though Lewis had some strong opponents among British churchmen, Anderson predicted that "in the years to come Lewis will be recognized as England's foremost champion of Christianity during those dark times that cried for a voice to reassure the people of the faith of the fathers."[36]

The most fascinating aspect of Lewis's early rise to fame in the United States is that although the mainstream press (such as the *New York Times*, *Time*, and the *Saturday Review*) and mainstream Protestants (who wrote for such publications) widely acclaimed him, American conservative evangelicals were very cautious in their praise. Their response was in that respect something like that of conservative Catholic commentators. But in this case the initial reserve is especially intriguing because eventually conservative evangelicals would most wholeheartedly embrace Lewis and practically canonize him.

In the 1940s American conservative evangelicals were usually known as "fundamentalists." At the time that was a broad designation for almost all revivalist-oriented groups and doctrinal conservatives, many of whom had engaged in sharp battles with modernists or theological liberals in the mainline Protestant churches. Some of these conflicts had led to church splits, and in any case fundamentalists in the north tended to operate in their own separate organizations. Most fundamentalists had strict behavioral rules, including prohibitions of smoking and drinking. They also had highly tuned antennae for detecting departures from their orthodoxies. So, for instance, the *Moody Monthly*, published by Moody Bible Institute, considered a sort of fundamentalist headquarters, praised *The Case for Christianity* as "another stimulating and thought-provoking book" and for its "trenchant" arguments against materialism and pantheism and for the divinity of Christ. But the review raised several flags of caution concerning what it saw as Lewis's "sacramentalism," his view of the Atonement, and his lack of certainty concerning the fate of those who did not know Christ.[37] The same magazine was somewhat more positive in a brief notice of *Christian Behaviour*, noting that in it Lewis "says a number of things with which one might take issue" but that he has "a sound Christian emphasis" and that "it is a book worth reading and rereading."[38] But, although conservative evangelicals liked Lewis for taking the Devil seriously in *The Screwtape Letters*, they simply did not give him a lot of attention in their publications. One notable exception was that in 1944 *His*, the magazine of InterVarsity Christian Fellowship, offered a several-page abridgement of passages from *Broadcast Talks*.[39] InterVarsity was a campus ministry with strong British ties, and this publication was a straw in the wind foretelling wide use of Lewis's work in campus evangelism.

One intellectual center of conservative evangelicals that gave Lewis's apologetics careful attention was Westminster Theological Seminary in Philadelphia, a stronghold for strictly orthodox Presbyterians, who saw themselves as guardians of traditional Christianity. The pattern was similar to that among American Jesuits: initial high praise and then backing away. Paul Woolley, a church historian, began a lengthy 1944 essay with the remark "C. S. Lewis is one of the finest reasons for giving thanks to God which the reviewer has met for some time." He characterized *The Case for Christianity* as "a brilliant statement" of basic reasons for being a Christian, and he found much to praise in *Christian Behaviour*. While careful to point out a number of doctrinal errors or infelicities in Lewis's work, Woolley concluded that "these volumes are the 'find' of the year for any literate Christian."[40]

With the appearance of *Beyond Personality*, in which Lewis explained his theology, a reaction set in. The *Westminster Theological Journal* published a largely negative review in 1946 by Jacob Dirk Eppinga, a young Christian Reformed minister.[41] Eppinga found Lewis's many mistakes all the more regrettable because "he can pack a greater wallop into one sentence than Joe Louis into a punch that starts from center-field." More consequentially, Westminster's own heavy-hitting apologist Cornelius Van Til at the same time (in May 1946) published a brief review in *United Evangelical Action*, the magazine of the leading conservative evangelical ecumenical group, the National Association of Evangelicals. Focusing on Lewis's distinction between making and begetting (the same passage that the Jesuits objected to), Van Til said that Lewis had blurred the distinction between the creator and creatures so that the volume was fatally flawed. "The evangelicalism that remains in a book of this sort is no more than incidental. The main argument of the book is destructive of evangelical faith."[42] Van Til was given to sweeping denunciations (he had just completed a book arguing that Karl Barth's neoorthodoxy was really "the new modernism"), but his word carried weight. In June 1946 *United Evangelical Action* published lists of "books of significance to evangelicals" and included *Beyond Personality* in the category of "volumes not evangelical in sentiment," describing it as "the Oxford don's stimulating but inadequate treatment of the Christian idea of God."[43]

Meanwhile, and in contrast to such evangelical ambivalence, Lewis's stock was only going up in mainstream postwar America as reviewers and the general public welcomed American editions of *The Great Divorce* (February 1946), *The Abolition of Man* (April

1947), and *Miracles* (September 1947). These represented the several fronts on which Lewis had been working as a Christian apologist. *The Great Divorce* was a fictional speculation on Heaven and Hell. *The Abolition of Man*, which had appeared in England in 1943, was a cultural critique of the philosophical-moral perspectives taught in British schools. And *Miracles* was his most technical defense of supernaturalism. One highlight of his steadily brightening American reputation was a feature article in the *Atlantic Monthly* in September 1946 by Chad Walsh, a professor of English at Beloit College in Wisconsin. Walsh, an Episcopalian, was becoming one of Lewis's leading American champions. His article "C. S. Lewis, Apostle to the Skeptics," was wholly laudatory, celebrating all of Lewis's books, which Walsh saw as part of "his one-man campaign to convert the world to Christianity." Walsh emphasized Lewis's orthodoxy and critiques of liberal theologies and observed that "the uncompromising and dogmatic Christianity that Lewis offers to the public has considerably more appeal than it would have had a few decades ago." Despite the persistence of the gospels of science and progress in America, others were questioning these. So "Lewis's morose suspicions of the worship of science seem less blasphemous today, since scientism is so intimately tied in with the religion of Progress that the two rise and fall together."[44]

Walsh spoke for many Protestants reared in the broad and inclusive theologies of the day, who were finding Lewis's undiluted supernaturalism refreshing. The most notable example of such an impact was that on the America Quaker theologian Elton Trueblood. Already an apologist for Christianity, he was chaplain and professor of the philosophy of religion at Stanford during the war years. Reading *The Screwtape Letters* and *The Case for Christianity* influenced him profoundly. Admiring Lewis's mastery at avoiding academic jargon, Trueblood "determined to try to do in America something of what C. S. Lewis was doing in England." Part of that involved writing small, accessible books that thoughtful laypeople might be likely to read. Trueblood admired Lewis for turning the tables by, rather than presenting Christianity from a defensive position, attacking the weakness of modern thought. Even more important, *The Case for Christianity* changed Trueblood's theological outlook. Particularly he found "unanswerable" Lewis's argument that Jesus could be just a "great moral teacher." No great moral teacher who was "merely a man" would make the outrageous claims about himself that Jesus did. That conviction helped turn Trueblood's theology in a more orthodox direction while he retained the progressive and pacifist moral emphases from his Quaker heritage. Trueblood, who taught for most of the rest of his career at Earlham, a Quaker college in Indiana, published a host of books on Christian themes and identified himself broadly with evangelicalism. He never met or corresponded with Lewis and always remained an independent thinker.[45]

In September 1947 Lewis achieved the nearest thing that American public life had to canonization as he appeared on the cover of *Time*. In an era when, despite the radio, print was the most authoritative way to reach mass audiences, *Time* was the supreme arbiter of middlebrow opinion. In America after the war, leading thinkers were debating whether recovery of its religious heritage might help save Western civilization from future debacles, especially from the threat of godless Communism.[46] In that setting, Henry Luce, publishing magnate and *Time* editor-in-chief, was a great promoter of the idea that America's greatness must rest on some sort of religious base. So *Time* framed the feature on Lewis in terms of the suggestion (which Chad Walsh had also made) that the twentieth-century secularist intellectual orthodoxy might be weakening. *Time* titled its article "Don v. Devil," and the cover pictured Lewis with an angel on one side and Screwtape on the other. The caption read: "Oxford's C. S. Lewis, His Heresy: Christianity." The article opened by depicting Lewis rushing out after a lecture to the nearest pub for "a pint of ale." It noted that "Lewis (like T. S. Eliot, W. H. Auden, et al.) is one of a growing band of heretics among modern intellectuals: an intellectual who believes in God." Lewis's fifteen books, said *Time*, had sold "something over a million copies." Among other things, the wide-ranging article noted that "Lewis is not particularly popular with his Oxford colleagues." It quoted one unnamed critic as having said Lewis's literary scholarship was "miles

CHAPTER THREE

ahead" of other such works, but as *Time* summarized, "in contrast to his tight scholarly writing (says this critic) Lewis' Christian propaganda is cheap sophism: having lured his reader onto the straight highway of logic, Lewis then inveigles him down the garden path of orthodox theology." *Time* closed with Lewis's observation that "Christianity is now 'on the map' among the younger intelligentsia, as it was not, say in 1920," but said that he also saw this current interest as a fashion that would likely fade as fashions do.[47]

In the wake of the *Time* cover story, Lewis's reputation continued to soar. In 1949 a reviewer in the *Los Angeles Times* could write, "C. S. Lewis is probably the most brilliant of all the Christian apologists of our time. Certainly he is the most widely read."[48] Later that year a reviewer in the *NYTBR*, surveying the upsurge in religious books, noted that what distinguished the current offerings was that they involved "top notch authors" as well as popularizers. Listing Lewis first, along with Graham Greene, W. H. Auden, Dorothy Sayers, Evelyn Waugh, Charles Williams, Arnold Toynbee, and T. S. Eliot, he asked, "Is it too much to say that never in recent centuries has the literature of England and America produced so large a body of successful religious writing, from both the literary and the theological point of view?"[49]

Even though many Americans of the World War II and postwar years would have rejected Lewis's Christian orthodoxy and even found it offensive, he does not seem to have been a divisive figure in American public life or among mainstream Protestants the way he was in Great Britain. He had not been a long-time polarizing radio presence in America. And Americans were typically ready to be impressed by sophisticated British accents and credentials. It also helped that Lewis did not fit any of the conventional American stereotypes. The United States did not have any leading intellectual community, such as Oxford, where sophisticated Catholics and Protestants might be allied. Lewis could offer mainstream American Protestantism (where anti-Roman prejudices were still often strong) catholic and traditionalist views, but he did not sound like a Roman Catholic. He viewed formulaic neo-Thomism, so popular among Roman Catholics of the day, as probably a passing fad.[50] He clearly was not a fundamentalist either, as the *Time* portrait signaled by starting with him rushing to a pub. In the American setting, Lewis was hard to pigeonhole and did not fit with any of the usual shorthand used to classify and dismiss.

Lewis's reputation in America was consolidated in 1949 by the first book about him, Chad Walsh's *C. S. Lewis: Apostle to the Skeptics*. Walsh had visited Lewis in Oxford in the summer of 1948. He observed that Lewis "still has no real conception of how widely his books are read and how familiarly his name is bandied about." Lewis, for instance, kept no scrapbook of reviews. Walsh found Lewis cordial and congenial. "When Lewis talks, he often reminds you of his books, particularly the broadcast talks. He is straight to the point, never at a loss for the exact word." Walsh set Lewis's popularity in the postwar context when many books with religious themes reached the bestseller lists. Whereas in previous decades it had been fashionable in literate circles to dismiss Christianity, people were questioning the directions in which secularism was leading Western civilization. Walsh called one of his chapters "'Mere Christianity,'" borrowing a term that Lewis had occasionally used but not yet as a title. Walsh also contrasted what he called Lewis's "classical Christianity" with the two outlooks that dominated American Protestant debates, "Modernist Christianity" and "Fundamentalist Christianity." Lewis frequently went out of his way to disparage modern liberal Christianity and in his doctrines was often closer to fundamentalism. Yet his classical Christianity also departed from fundamentalism in that he was open to taking some of the Old Testament accounts, such as the story of the Garden of Eden, as not literal. So he did not invite warfare with science over biological evolution, even if he was critical of scientism.[51]

# A Classic as Afterthought

Already by 1947, when the *Time* cover and article appeared, Lewis was at the end of an era. During the war Lewis had written a remarkable number of books, eleven in all. Some of these were still coming out in 1946 and 1947, but Lewis's activities had changed dramatically. The *Time* article reported that Oxford's postwar "swollen enrollment" was keeping Lewis busy and that he was devoting his spare time to work on his volume for "Oh Hell," his shorthand for the *Oxford History of English Literature* (*OHEL*). The reporter also noted that he had told the BBC that he was "through with radiorat-ing, for an indefinite period," and he had no immediate plans for further popular books.[1]

As the comment about "radiorat-ing" suggested, Lewis had already put behind him the sort of popular apologetics and evangelism he had engaged in for the RAF and the broadcast talks. He had taken those on as part of his war service to the nation. But popular evangelism was immensely time-consuming. It swelled the volume of his already often overwhelming correspondence. He had done what he could for the occasion, but as soon as the war ended he was ready for others to take over the task. As he wrote just after the war in response to a request to write a book for factory workers, not only did he "know nothing at all of the realities of factory life," but also others should be as able as he was to take on such tasks. He explained, as he often did, that he simply acted as "a translator." Yet many people might learn to do that. "People praise me as a 'translator', but what I want is to be the founder of a school of translation." "I am nearly forty-seven," Lewis lamented already in 1945. "Where are my successors?"[2]

Lewis also found apologetic work spiritually debilitating. "I have found that nothing is more dangerous to one's own faith," he told a group of Anglican clergy and youth workers in 1945, "than the work of an apologist. No doctrine of that Faith seems to me so spectral, so unreal as one that I have just successfully defended in a public debate." The problem, he explained, was that such occasions make the doctrine appear to rest on the "weak pillar" of one's own self and arguments. Faith could not rest just on cold reasoning. One needed to get back "into the Reality—from Christian apologetic into Christ himself."[3]

When Lewis made these observations in the spring of 1945, he was in the late stages of writing what would prove to be his last directly apologetic work, *Miracles: A Preliminary Study*. Dorothy Sayers has suggested that he do a book on that topic in 1943, and by May

1945 he was reporting to Sister Penelope that it was finished. For unknown reasons (perhaps because readers had suggested revisions), it did not appear until May of 1947.[4] *Miracles* was not designed to be a popular book. Rather, it involved careful philosophical arguments in defense of belief in supernaturalism as opposed to modern naturalism. As the *Time* article indicated, Lewis's academic obligations at Oxford had greatly increased. He continued to face pressures from colleagues who resented his Christian popularizing. In the postwar years his Oxford friends, especially J.R.R. Tolkien, were hoping that Lewis would be elected to one of several prestigious professorships. A principal obstacle was opposition from colleagues who objected that his Christian proselytizing was unprofessional. "You don't know how much I am hated," he once remarked with great feeling to a younger friend.[5] Those concerns provided all the more reason to devote his serious writing time to "Oh Hell." So neither any more popular nor any more professional apologetics works were on the horizon.

In the summer of 1948, Lewis turned to writing the Narnia books in his spare time. He had already started a spiritual autobiography but put that aside (it would appear as *Surprised by Joy* in 1955) in favor of writing children's books. That was something Lewis had first attempted but abandoned in 1939. Getting any such extracurricular writing done had been difficult in the immediate postwar years. In addition to his increased academic duties, he had to deal with Minto, who was seriously failing in both body and mind and was increasingly demanding of his presence and care. In the summer of 1948, the family finally moved her into a nursing home, where she would remain until her death in 1951. Lewis took up his new project in the summer of 1948, and by the end of the year he had written *The Lion, The Witch, and the Wardrobe*.[6]

The story of Lewis's turn to writing *Narnia* is relevant to that of *Mere Christianity* in a couple of respects. First, the satisfaction and success in writing children's novels reinforced a decision already made not to engage in any new popular works that were explicitly apologetic. There was not going to be a fifth series of broadcast talks. So it made sense to collect and publish together what there was. Second, eventually Lewis would be better known for *Narnia* than for anything else. Once that happened, no matter how popular *Mere Christianity* would be, as a publication it would always sail in the wake of *Narnia*. Many people who first encountered Lewis as a favorite children's author would be prepared to look on him favorably as someone worth reading as an adult. Just as the radio broadcasts started out with *praeparatio evangelica*, the Narnia books served as a preparation for that preparation, introducing children to a world that had many of the features of a Christian universe.

One speculation, now widely dismissed, is that Lewis's turn from apologetics to children's books resulted from a momentous public defeat in a debate with a brilliant young philosopher, Elizabeth

Anscombe, in February 1948. Lewis was the president of the Socratic Club at Oxford from 1942 to 1954. The Socratic Club sponsored public discussions and debates on religious and philosophical issues, often between Christians and non-Christians. Lewis was known to be a formidable debater, skilled in both logic and rhetoric. On this occasion Anscombe, herself a Catholic, presented a paper criticizing Lewis's argument in chapter 3 of *Miracles* that naturalism was self-refuting. If naturalism (in the sense of excluding the supernatural) were true, Lewis had argued, human thought would be based on irrational causes and hence one would have no basis for concluding that one's arguments for naturalism itself were valid. Anscombe, who was trained in modern analytic philosophy, pointed out that Lewis had blurred some essential distinctions, such as between "irrational" and "non-rational" and the meanings of "valid" and "invalid." Lewis responded, and the exchange was subsequently published, but Lewis came away with a sense that he had been soundly defeated. That Anscombe was a woman possibly added to his chagrin. Nonetheless, he continued to defend his central point and carefully revised the chapter for a later edition of *Miracles*, taking Anscombe's technical suggestions into account.[7] As biographer Alan Jacobs concludes in an insightful overview of the controversy, "Whatever changes took place in Lewis's career at this time, the debate with Anscombe could have played but a minor part, if indeed it played any part at all, in their emergence."[8] The fact is that Lewis had not been involved in any new apologetic works since he had finished his draft of *Miracles* in the spring of 1945. Michael Ward, in *Planet Narnia*, argues persuasively that in the Narnia books Lewis, rather than retreating, was recasting his argument against naturalism in imaginative form.[9]

Nonetheless, the Anscombe story, even if sometimes greatly overblown in other respects, did have a direct impact on *Mere Christianity* that seems not to have been noticed. When Lewis combined the three earlier publications, he made only a few substantial revisions. One that he did make was in the first chapter of book 2, *What Christians Believe*. In the second paragraph, which now says simply that "the first big division of humanity" is between the majority, who believe in some kind of God or gods, and "the modern Western European materialist" minority. In revising, Lewis quietly eliminated the rest of the paragraph that in *Broadcast Talks* reads as follows:

> There are all sorts of different reasons for believing in God and here I'll mention only one. It is this. Supposing there was no intelligence behind the universe, no creative mind. In that case nobody designed my brain for the purpose of thinking. It is merely that when the atoms inside my skull happen from physical or chemical reasons to arrange themselves in a certain way, this gives me, as a bye-product, the sensation I call thought. But if so, how can I trust my

own thinking to be true? It's like upsetting a milk-jug and hoping that the way the splash arranges itself will give you a map of London. But if I can't trust my own thinking, of course, I can't trust the arguments leading to atheism, and therefore have no reason to be an atheist, or anything else. Unless I believe in God, I can't believe in thought: so I can never use thought to disbelieve in God.[10]

This is a significant passage. It bears on an argument still going on today as to whether Lewis assumed a naïve Enlightenment view of universal reason.[11] As the revision of *Miracles* shows, he did not abandon his argument, but after the Anscombe debate he apparently had concluded that the popular formulation regarding reason for the broadcast talk had been too sweeping and imprecise.

Whose idea was it to combine the three small books from the broadcasts into what became *Mere Christianity*? No one knows. No correspondence or other indication that would answer that question seems to survive. The editing and revision required for this new edition was not a major project for Lewis, so it is not surprising that he did not comment on it. *Mere Christianity* first appeared in England from publisher Geoffrey Bles on July 7, 1952, and in America from Macmillan on November 11, 1952.[12] The full title was *Mere Christianity: A Revised and Enlarged Edition, with a New Introduction of the Three Books*, Broadcast Talks, Christian Behaviour, *and* Beyond Personality. For a number of years each of these original works remained in print along with the combined edition, and, as the cumbersome full title suggests, Lewis wanted to be sure no one thought *Mere Christianity* was a new book. He later chided a publisher for listing the original three volumes as well as *Mere Christianity* as among his works, lest buyers might be "stung" by buying something they already had.[13]

The preeminent new additions to the combined edition were the new title, *Mere Christianity*, and Lewis's exposition of his meaning for that phrase in a substantial new preface. Lewis had used the term already in *The Screwtape Letters*, where Screwtape laments that Wormwood's patient has fallen in with a set of friends who practice "mere Christianity." Their commitments would be much more susceptible to subversion, says the senior devil, if they emphasized "Christianity And," things like "Christianity and the New Order," or "Christianity and Faith Healing," or "Christianity and Vegetarianism." The antidote he offers is "Substitute for the faith itself some Fashion with a Christian colouring. Work on their horror of the Same Old Thing."[14] Lewis used the term again in 1944 in an introduction to a new translation by his friend Sister Penelope of Saint Athanasius's *The Incarnation of the Word of God*. Once again he warned against being taken in by untested faddish modern views of Christianity: "The only safety is to have a standard of plain, central Christianity ('mere Christianity' as Baxter called it) which puts the controversies of the moment in their proper perspective. Such a standard can be acquired only from old books."[15]

Richard Baxter (1615–91) was an English preacher and prolific writer who suffered greatly in an era of intense sectarian controversy, warfare, and religious repression. He was a moderate theologically and politically but sided with Oliver Cromwell during the English Civil Wars and the Puritan Commonwealth in the middle decades of the century. Even though he was an inveterate peacemaker who helped with the restoration of the monarchy in 1660, he was subsequently barred from ecclesiastical office and also imprisoned for eighteen months. His greatest influence was through his writings, including the classic devotional work *The Saints' Everlasting Rest* and the long-used evangelistic appeal *A Call to the Unconverted*.

In that context Baxter described his own moderate position in a 1681 work:

> I am a CHRISTIAN, a MEER CHRISTIAN, of no other Religion; and the Church that I am of is the Christian Church, and hath been visible where ever the Christian Religion and Church hath been visible: But must you know what Sect or Party I am of? I am against all Sects and dividing Parties: But if any will call Meer Christians by the name of a Party, because they take up with Meer Christianity, Creed, and Scripture, and will not be of any dividing or contentious Sect, I am of that Party which is so against Parties.[16]

Lewis used his new preface to elaborate on his own meaning for the term in what has become one of the most often-cited parts of *Mere Christianity*. Of the original publications, only the first and the third volumes had brief prefaces. In *Broadcast Talks* (*The Case for Christianity*), Lewis began with an explanation he had given on the air: "I gave these talks, not because I am anyone in particular, but because I was asked to do so. I think they asked me chiefly for two reasons: firstly, because I am a layman, not a clergyman; and secondly, because I had been a non-Christian for many years." He went on to explain that although he was in the Church of England himself, he had vetted the second series of talks with clergymen of four differing denominations and that, despite minor differences, they agreed. So he believed that one could take the second series as "plain Christianity that no Christian disagrees with."[17] In the preface to *Beyond Personality* he reiterated that he was attempting "to put into simple modern language the account of God which, to the best of my knowledge, the vast majority of Christian churches have agreed in giving for a great many centuries." He said that, although he believed these doctrines himself, he was not dictating what was "Christian" and what was not, other then to describe what in fact was "the central tradition" of Christianity. Still less was he setting a standard by which to judge whose heart was truly "Christian," because only God could judge that.[18]

The new preface expanded on these sorts of points much more systematically. The book, Lewis explained, would be of "no help to anyone who is hesitating between two Christian 'denominations.'" He went on to affirm that he was "not writing to expound something I could call 'my religion,' but to expound 'mere Christianity, which is what it is and what it was long before I was born and whether I like it or not.'" And although these doctrines could be found in *The Book of Common Prayer*, they were not "anything that was peculiar to the Church of England." He also expanded at considerable length his point from the earlier preface that he was not judging who was "Christian" in the sense of being a good person or having a heart that was right with God. "Mere Christianity," he emphasized, was not minimalist, lowest-common-denominator Christianity. Rather than being "vague and bloodless," it turned out to be "something not only positive but pungent." Even so, Lewis's much-cited concluding point was that people should not think of "mere Christianity" as a substitute for specific denominational affiliation. "Mere Christianity," he explained in one of his memorable metaphors, "is more like a hall out of which doors open into several rooms. If I can bring anyone into that hall I have done what I attempted. But it is in the rooms, not in the hall, that there are fires and chairs and meals." The hall, he continued, is only a place to wait, not a place to live. Eventually one would have to choose a particular room, a particular church. Having said that, Lewis closed, extending the metaphor on a wonderfully irenic note: "When you have reached your own room, be kind to those who have chosen different doors and to those who are still in the hall. If they are wrong they need your prayers all the more; and if they are your enemies, then you are under orders to pray for them. That is one of the rules common to the whole house."

Lewis remarked to one inquirer that the new combined edition contained "important corrections."[19] Nevertheless, these seem to have been remarkably few. Of the handful of substantial changes in the first two books, the largest was the addition of two paragraphs in book 2, chapter 3, "The Shocking Alternative." These had to do with what became Lewis's most famous argument: that Jesus was either "the Son of God: or else a madman or something worse." He could not be a "great moral teacher" and have made the claims he did. The new paragraphs elaborated on Jesus's astonishing claim that he could forgive people's sins and that, at the same time, he could have appeared, as he claimed, "'humble and meek.'" This overall argument, which continues to persuade readers but attract critics, had already been a focus of criticism in reviews.[20]

The other larger changes came in book 3, *Christian Behaviour*, in the chapters titled "Sexual Morality" and "Christian Marriage," also topics that had been the focus of some criticisms. Regarding sexual morality, Lewis added a long first paragraph, appropriate to the changing public mores of the postwar era, pointing out that the Christian virtue of chastity should not be confused with changing social rules of "modesty." Christians, he said, would not necessarily have to be old-fashioned in their standards for public dress and behavior. He also added a couple of pages defending the idea that the practice of Christian chastity was feasible in the modern world. In "Christian Marriage" he added two paragraphs regarding justice as an important consideration in honoring one's marriage vows. He also expanded what had been a single paragraph into a couple of pages on the inadequacy of "being in love" as the supreme justification for marriage. He let book 4, *Beyond Personality*, in contrast to the other sections, stand virtually as in the original, excepting that he changed the subtitle from *The Christian Idea of God* to the more modest *First Steps in the Doctrine of the Trinity*. See the appendix for a full review of notable changes.

# Into the Evangelical Orbit

*Mere Christianity* emerged as a single volume with no trumpets and fanfare. Because it was a collection and a print version of Lewis's well-known radio broadcasts, it received virtually no reviews. It steadily sold well in its early years and seems to have gained momentum, as indicated by its new printings more or less every year in both Great Britain and the United States and by its going into paperback editions.[1] Still, despite its always strong sales, *Mere Christianity* remained unobtrusive among the author's many works. Lewis was still typically presented as "The Author of *The Screwtape Letters*."

In England Lewis remained a controversial figure. Novelist and critic Kathleen Nott, for instance, published *The Emperor's Clothes* in 1953, in which she sharply attacked the idea that Western civilization might be saved by a return to the "dogmatic orthodoxy" of writers such as T. S. Eliot, C. S. Lewis, and Dorothy Sayers. The strength of Western civilization, Nott argued to the contrary, was to be found in humanism, which cultivated individual freedom, the arts, and scientific inquiry. Nott preferred the sophisticated Eliot to Lewis and Sayers because she thought the latter were too ready to argue about any theological issue and did so with "a certain vulgarity, like the Salvation Army." These writers, she opined, "could be described, not too metaphorically, as fundamentalists" in the sense that they held that all the answers humans need could be found in Christian revelation and church teachings.[2]

Although Lewis, especially when he moved in academic circles, often encountered such disparagements of his popular apologetics, he was also reaching the pinnacle of his scholarly reputation. Enemies at Oxford had blocked his appointment to a chair there, but Cambridge University recognized his eminence as a literary critic in 1954 by appointing him to a new professorship in Medieval and Renaissance studies.

Even so, Lewis was still best known as a popular Christian apologist. In the spring of 1955, Tom Driberg, a prominent journalist and left-wing Labour member of Parliament who was also a High-Church Anglican, wrote of Lewis's role in connection with the much-heralded revival of religion, or at least of "interest in religion" in England. Billy Graham had conducted a remarkably successful three-month revival campaign in London early in 1954, preaching to some huge crowds, and he was to return in 1955. The vogue of Graham's conversionist message may have had something to do with the Collins company's issuing a Fontana Books mass-market paperback edition of *Mere Christianity* in 1955. In any case, citing *Mere Christianity* and *The Screwtape Letters*, Driberg described Lewis in the *New Statesman and Nation* as "the most popular theologian of the day." He recognized that Lewis was "not a fundamentalist" in the biblical literalist sense, as Graham was. Nonetheless, he saw the two as similar in that they largely ignored the "social gospel" in favor of an individualistic message of salvation of souls for eternal life. Driberg pointed out that Lewis had said in *Mere Christianity*, "'A Christian society is not going to arrive until most of us really want it; and we are not going to want it until we become fully Christian.'" And Driberg saw that as a "comfortable excuse for doing nothing to change society."[3]

In the United States Lewis was looked upon as a more mainstream religious figure and had drawn far less public criticism than he had received in England ever since his controversial wartime broadcasts. Lewis sustained his popularity in America despite making no secret of his disdain for the superficialities of American culture and religion. Many Americans, perhaps sensing that same superficiality, found his historically grounded depth refreshing and became his most ardent admirers. Americans, including a number of American women, were among his most thoughtful correspondents, and eventually, in 1956, he married one of these, Joy Davidman.

Another American admirer, Chad Walsh, as the author of the first book on Lewis, spent lots of time with

Lewis's followers during the early 1950s and later identified several types of people attracted to Lewis's centrist style of traditional Christianity. Among these were those who were discontent with various kinds of theological liberalism and so found Lewis helpful as they were groping their way to, or perhaps back to, Christian orthodoxy. Then there were those who were reacting against the "super-orthodox" or "obscurantist fundamentalist" churches they had been brought up in and were looking for an intellectually viable faith in the "main Christian tradition." Walsh noted that Lewis's works "were particularly popular with clergy on the intellectual firing line—for example, college and university chaplains." These, he said, sometimes bought Lewis's books "by the gross in order to give them to eager young intellectuals who were disturbed by religious questions." There were also those who remained "outright 'Fundamentalists'" and "welcomed Lewis as an ally," although "many regretted that he was not specific enough about the inerrancy of the Scriptures." Finally, Walsh found, "surprisingly, or perhaps not surprisingly," that Lewis had "a large following among Roman Catholics." He observed that "though many Roman Catholics would wish that Lewis had gone farther at a number of points they seem to find little to criticize in what he said as far as he went." Catholic admirers liked his "fresh and vital restatements of the doctrines they learned more drily in Catechism."[4]

By the later 1950s, especially due to the influence of Billy Graham, it was apparent that evangelical

Protestants were making a comeback in American Protestantism. Ever since the Scopes "Monkey Trial" of 1925, mainstream Protestants and other cultural leaders had often dismissed them as "fundamentalists," but Graham was helping to lead revivalist Christianity back into the cultural mainstream. He and his allies were now calling themselves "new evangelicals" and seeking influence in the halls of power, cooperation with mainline Protestantism, and intellectual respectability. For them, Lewis could be a useful ally. Recognizing that, Billy Graham himself had consulted Lewis in 1955 in connection with a campaign Graham was conducting at Cambridge University. Lewis later said that he had been impressed with Graham as "a very modest and a very sensible man and I liked him very much indeed."[5] Nonetheless, he kept his distance from public identification with American-style revivalism.

As in England, Graham's popular successes led to a perceived link between his conversionist message and Lewis's, and so to some outright attacks on Lewis. Graham reached a new peak with his New York Crusade of 1957 and was cooperating with local mainline Protestant churches. Around the same time, the *Christian Century*, guardian of progressive Protestantism, offered a series of attacks on Graham as representing the old fundamentalism in disguise.[6] Norman Pittenger, a professor of apologetics at General Theological Seminary in New York, had already linked Lewis to Graham, proclaiming that Lewis's popularity was "one of the danger signs of our time" in "presenting the Christian religion in its most incredible form with glibness and a specious appeal."[7] In 1958 the *Christian Century*, which had until then been largely positive regarding Lewis, published Pittenger's detailed indictment of the British "defender of the faith."[8]

Pittenger began by noting that Lewis was "the best known and most admired" apologist of the day and that *Mere Christianity* had "had an enormous sale" in both Great Britain and America and "had tremendous influence." He also conceded that Lewis was a master storyteller and that the *Narnia* tales were "altogether charming." But he deplored the fact that Lewis was being taken seriously as a contemporary theologian. He had "even seen" Lewis's works "cited in scholarly tomes as authoritative discussions." Moreover, due to Lewis's cleverness and brilliance as a writer, "it seems to be fashion nowadays to quote Mr. Lewis as if he were one of the church fathers." Even though Lewis's broadcast talks had doubtless helped many "as their first introduction to Christian faith as a live option for intelligent people today," these people needed to be warned that he was an "amateur theologian" who misunderstood even the orthodoxy he claimed to defend and was woefully disregardful of modern standards of biblical interpretation.[9]

Lewis's popular apologetics in *Mere Christianity*, Pittenger warned, combined "crudity" with dogmatism based on simplistic understandings of the "authority" of biblical and church teachings. So, for example,

Pittenger regarded Lewis's illustration of the Trinity as "'like a cube' that is 'six squares while remaining one cube'" as an "inept illustration" that made Pittenger "doubt if Lewis really grasps the doctrine of the Trinity in its classical sense." Pittenger also depicted Lewis's argument that Jesus must be either God or a lunatic as seemingly clever, but said "it is really only vulgar." That Lewis took New Testament accounts of Jesus's claims simply at face value, rather than as being refracted through the faith of the Apostles and Gospel writers, illustrated his failure to interpret Scripture "in the light of the best critical analysis." All in all, Lewis was, even if brilliant and clever, "a dangerous apologist and an inept theologian."[10]

Pittenger's condescending polemic awakened Lewis from his apologetic slumbers. He had earlier said that it was almost always a mistake to answer criticisms, but within weeks he sent the *Christian Century* an article in rebuttal in which he pulled out the stops in his display of debating skills. After conceding a few technical points, Lewis went on the counterattack. Pittenger's style of biblical interpretation and his resulting theological claims had a confusing ambiguity about them. As for defending Lewis's own theology in his broadcasts, Lewis pointed out that Pittenger failed to interpret them in *their own* context, as being directed to popular, not academic, audiences. Perhaps Lewis's use of geometry to illustrate the Holy Trinity had been vulgar and offensive. "I could have understood the Doctor's being shocked," wrote Lewis with ironical flourish, "if I had compared God to an unjust judge or Christ to a thief in the night; but mathematical objects seem to me as free from sordid associations as any the mind can entertain."[11]

Lewis explained that prior to his broadcasts, "Christianity came before the great mass of my unbelieving fellow-countrymen either in the highly emotional form offered by revivalists or in the unintelligible language of highly cultured clergy." Neither of these reached most people, so he had undertaken the task of being a "*translator*," putting Christian doctrine into the vernacular. For such a purpose a more nuanced style, "more rich in fruitful ambiguities—in fact, a style more like Dr. Pittenger's own—would have been worse than useless." The reader "would have thought, poor soul, that I was facing both ways, sitting on the fence, offering at one moment what I withdrew the next, and generally trying to trick him."[12]

The exchange with Pittenger marked a turning point in Lewis's public reputation as an apologist, especially among American evangelicals with fundamentalist backgrounds. Ever since *The Screwtape Letters*, many such conservative evangelicals had been discovering Lewis. Already in 1943, in a significant example, Clyde Kilby, on the English faculty of Wheaton College in Illinois, had picked up *The Case for Christianity* in the college bookstore and thrilled to its refreshing tone. Wheaton College, Billy Graham's alma mater, was at the time the leading fundamentalist college. It was also an academic center that was

CHAPTER FIVE

shaping what would soon become the "new evangelical" movement. Lewis did not fit with this fundamentalistic heritage in a number of ways: he smoked and drank, did not hold to biblical "inerrancy," and was open to theistic evolution. Yet new evangelicals welcomed his unabashed affirmations of the supernatural and his nonsectarianism, which connected the faith to teachings of the church through the ages.[13]

In 1956 Graham and others helped launch a new thought journal, *Christianity Today*, designed to rival the *Christian Century*. Already in 1955, Carl F. H. Henry, editor of the new magazine, had asked Lewis if he might be a contributor. Lewis politely replied, "I wish your project heartily well but can't write you articles." He went on to explain that he had turned to fiction and symbol as his modes of Christian expression. "I do not think I am at all likely to write more *directly* theological pieces." He added, "I have done what I could in the way of frontal attacks, but I now feel quite sure those days are over."[14] This was the sort of reply that one writes if one not only is turning down a request but also does not wish to leave the door open for the future solicitations. Lewis was exaggerating a bit his resolve not to write directly Christian prose reflections for general audiences. He had often expressed his suspicions of revivalist Americans, and apparently he still wanted to keep them at a bit of a distance.

The Pittenger review had the unintended consequence of pushing Lewis closer toward this American evangelical orbit. Clyde Kilby sent Lewis a copy of the

Pittenger article, along with a rebuttal that Kilby had sent to the *Christian Century* as a possible reply. Lewis answered that the *Christian Century* had already sent him the Pittenger piece and had offered to print his response. Lewis said he hoped they might publish both responses but added that "alas, we may merely be putting up the sales of what seems a pretty nasty periodical!"[15] Kilby then sent his article to *Christianity Today*. Carl Henry promptly published it and also sent Lewis a copy to see if Lewis would also like to provide a rejoinder to Pittenger for *Christianity Today*. Lewis told Henry that if the *Christian Century* should turn down his response, he would be happy to have *Christianity Today* publish it.[16]

Kilby's strong and unreserved defense of Lewis in *Christianity Today* sent up a flag that American evangelicals were claiming Lewis versus mainline Protestant theologians, whom evangelicals saw as undermining the historic faith. Even if Lewis remained reluctant to be pulled into such circles, evangelical leaders recognized that his combination of academic credentials and orthodoxy fit their purposes of reestablishing intellectual credibility for conservative Protestantism.

Thanks in part to the efforts of Graham and *Christianity Today*, American evangelicals, along with some crucial British allies, were building an international network in which Lewis the apologist was to play a significant role. One key figure was the British theologian J. I. Packer, for whom Lewis's published radio talks had been important in shaping his faith in the 1940s. Packer was a prominent contributor to *Christianity Today*, and his *Fundamentalism and the Word of God* was a widely read defense of traditional Christianity affirming the inerrancy of Scripture. Similarly influential in building a British-American evangelical network with intellectual credibility was John R. Stott, the rector of All Souls Church in London from 1950 to 1975. During his university days, Stott had been a leader in the Cambridge Inter-Collegiate Christian Union, and as an organizer of Billy Graham's campaign there in 1955, he had personally brought Graham and Lewis together in their meeting that year. In subsequent decades, Stott became the preeminent figure working with Graham in building immense worldwide networks of evangelical Christians. Stott also authored *Basic Christianity* (1958), a popular apologetic volume that might be seen as complementing *Mere Christianity*. Stott's approach was more straightforward and conventional, presenting a basic primer of Christian teaching, starting with Scripture's claims regarding the divinity of Christ and then moving on to the implications of Christ's saving work. *Basic Christianity* long has rivaled *Mere Christianity* in popularity, having sold more than two million copies and been translated into more than sixty languages.[17] In it Stott puts *Mere Christianity* first among "good Christian books" that he urges his audience to read.[18]

In his later years Lewis was convinced that his works would soon be forgotten. Shortly before his death in 1963, he told his friend Owen Barfield he expected that his fame would quickly pass and that within five years no one would be reading his books. Lewis made that pessimistic prediction despite the fact that up to that time his books had sold about a million copies in paperback alone. *Mere Christianity* was very prominent among these, accounting for about a quarter of that total, just slightly ahead of *The Screwtape Letters*. At the time, the Narnia books, although highly regarded and selling well, were not Lewis's best-known works, let alone iconic (the *New York Times* obituary misspelled them as the "Chronicles of Narvia").[19] And Lewis had continued to write, in addition to his fiction and literary criticism, other books for Christian audiences, such as *Reflections on the Psalms* (1958), *The Four Loves* (1960), and *Letters to Malcolm: Chiefly on Prayer* (1964), though none had the impact of his works of the 1940s.

As the postwar era gave way to the 1960s, there was reason to think that a book such as *Mere Christianity* would not last. Whatever Lewis had thought of the subject, that was the opinion of Chad Walsh in 1965. Lewis, he believed, "is entering into a period of relative obscurity." Even as Walsh recounted Lewis's wide popularity in America, he thought that was largely a phenomenon that had reached its peak in the early 1950s and wrote that "it is simply that he is less talked about than ten or fifteen years ago." The period from World War II into the later 1950s had been a time of Christian renewal throughout the English-speaking world, but now that was fading. Furthermore, by 1964 or 1965 a revolution in public culture was looming. Walsh, who taught at Beloit College in Wisconsin, found that "among college students I hear much less talk about religion than ten years ago." If students were religious, they were not so much concerned with questions of truth or falsity as with relevance. So they might be interested in the Peace Corps or promoting interracial justice. "To such young people Lewis seems much too theoretical and abstract," he wrote. Walsh believed that a mood of "diffused existentialism" characterized most young people in the America of the 1960s. So they found Lewis "too much a rationalist and Thomist for their tastes." Therefore, even though Walsh was confident that Lewis's fiction would last, his "own prediction for what it is worth" was that "his straightforward books, such as *Broadcast Talks*, will not last forever. They were splendid religious journalism, but each age should produce its own journalists."[20]

Lewis was at least out of the limelight during the turbulent years of the later 1960s, when political causes, cultural upheaval, sexual revolutions, indulgent individualism, new-age spirituality, and just about everything but his unobtrusive "mere Christianity" came to the fore in public culture. Nonetheless, his literary executor, Walter Hooper, a devoted American admirer who had served briefly as Lewis's secretary in 1963, worked assiduously to keep Lewis's works in print and to bring out previously unpublished writings. According to Hooper, "I made clear that Collins [the publisher] would get a new Lewis book on the condition they reprinted two books that had gone out of print. It was tough going at first, but eventually they understood that Lewis would be around for a long time."[21] Peter Kreeft, who became an influential Roman Catholic promoter of Lewis, similarly reported that in the later 1960s, when he first proposed a book on Lewis, his publisher said, "'We think Lewis' star has risen and is about to set. His day is over. No one will be reading C. S. Lewis twenty years from now.'"[22] In 1970, in *The Christian Century*, in a brief unsigned notice of *God in the Dock*, a collection of Lewis essays edited by Hooper, the reviewer observed, "It is too early for a C. S. Lewis revival and too late to capitalize on the C. S. Lewis fad."[23]

Yale theologian Paul Holmer's volume *C. S. Lewis: The Shape of His Faith and Thought* represented a late flowering of mainline Protestant interest in Lewis.[24] Not published until 1976, it had the feel of a retrospective tribute to a figure from the past who was still worth looking at. "Lewis," wrote Holmer, "was from the early years of World War II through the mid-fifties the most widely read Christian apologist in English." Holmer explained that his own book was "written partly to discharge a debt incurred during the early days of World War II." As a young man Holmer had been struggling as a fundamentalist, and Lewis's correspondence with him had helped him untangle his life and broaden his faith. Holmer's volume has the feel of having been drafted in the earlier era. For instance, when he refers to Lewis's most popular books he lists *The Case for Christianity* rather than *Mere Christianity* and cites the latter as such only in a couple of notes instructing the reader to "see" its "new Preface."[25]

Although Holmer's tribute may have been long in the making, that also meant that the Yale professor had had years of reflection and teaching to hone his insights, so his volume remains a classic for understanding Lewis's strengths as a popular defender of Christianity. Holmer considered Lewis's fiction and literary criticism as integrally related to his ability to speak to broad audiences. He also noted how deeply Lewis's thought was shaped not only by perennial Christianity but also by the whole span of Western civilization and by his lifelong attention to understanding perennial human nature. Those perspectives gave him "a rare wisdom about people" so that "his writings have a way of fitting every reader."[26] Few writers, Holmer observed, combined the objective and the subjective so well as Lewis had done, so that readers come to realize that they are not just learning about the faith but also learning something about themselves. Lewis wrote with the authority of someone who had discovered something and could convey an artful simplicity that fit with the experiences of many others who find it a way of making sense of their lives.[27]

If by the time Holmer's book appeared in 1976 Lewis's popularity as an apologist seemed to have faded in American mainline Protestant circles, just the opposite had happened among American evangelicals. In fact, the most dramatic trend in the story of the reception *Mere Christianity* is that of its rise from being just well liked to iconic status during that relatively brief span of time.

Clyde Kilby had emerged in the late 1950s as the chief evangelical advocate for Lewis, and in 1964 he consolidated that status with his defense of Lewis, *The Christian World of C. S. Lewis*. Kilby, who was a literary scholar, offered an overview of and introduction to the whole corpus of Lewis's work. What he said directly in summarizing *Mere Christianity* was probably less significant for the future life of that book than who was saying it—a respected professor at the most elite college in the evangelical orbit. Moreover, Kilby's personal influence among Wheaton students was sufficient to ensure that, in the 1960s, whatever was happening at other colleges, such as Beloit or Berkeley, the future leaders of American evangelicalism, including many of its intellectual leaders, were going to have a high regard for Lewis. Wheaton was also a leading institution in defining the boundaries of evangelical orthodoxy. So it mattered that a Wheaton professor was pointing out that, even if Lewis did not hold to the "inerrancy" of Scripture, a doctrine that was often used as a test of fellowship by conservative evangelicals, he had a high view of the historicity of the New Testament and had little time for modern biblical criticism. Furthermore, even though Lewis stood "somewhat to the left" of many orthodox Christians on that and some other matters, he stood firmly against liberal theologies and in defense of essential traditional doctrines and of the miraculous versus modern naturalistic skepticism.[28]

Kilby cemented the relationship between evangelicalism's leading college and Lewis by establishing there in 1965 a "C. S. Lewis Collection." By the time of Kilby's retirement in 1981, that had grown into a well-funded major research archive, the Marion E. Wade Center. Located on Wheaton's campus, the Center signaled the American evangelical embrace not only of Lewis but also of Lewis's kindred British literary allies from diverse Christian traditions, including Owen Barfield, G. K. Chesterton, George MacDonald, Dorothy Sayers, J.R.R. Tolkien, and Charles Williams. The Center has also gathered some artifacts, including the original Lewis wardrobe that was the inspiration for that in *The Lion, the Witch, and the Wardrobe*. Standing across the campus from the architecturally dominant Billy Graham Center, the Wade Center helped make Wheaton a destination where evangelicals might honor Lewis in its hierarchy of saints.

Even more influential, although difficult to measure, was Lewis's influence on evangelical leaders who had discovered him, usually during their student years. At any gathering of prominent evangelicals, some will have such stories. Particularly important in promoting Lewis on campuses was InterVarsity Christian Fellowship. InterVarsity had close ties to counterparts in British universities where Lewis's apologetic works were often used in evangelism. As early as the 1940s, Gene Thomas, who became a highly influential leader of InterVarsity Christian Fellowship in Colorado, discovered *The Case for*

*Christianity* through a recommendation in that organization's *His* magazine.[29] Another typical story is that of Terry Morrison, who was long the director of Inter-Varsity faculty ministries. Morrison was introduced to Lewis as a student in Pittsburgh in the early 1950s from reading an early edition of *Mere Christianity*. Soon he was reading everything by Lewis that he could find and promoting him with others. According to Morrison, "A good many of our staff, at least through the 1970s, were brought to the Lord after reading Lewis." He said that many of the staff counted Lewis as "extremely important for our work," and "a good many students were nourished on Lewis." Lewis became standard fare in dorm discussions, and over the years InterVarsity Press has offered a steady diet of books about him. The press's publisher, Bob Fryling, remarks, "Outside of the Scriptures themselves, Lewis is probably the greatest authority and example of a thoughtful Christian faith. In a university environment, Lewis has stellar academic credentials that command intellectual respect, while his journey from atheism to Christian faith describes a personal and spiritual authority that is attractive and not easily dismissed."[30]

Such influences had many ripple effects, and by at least the end of the 1960s Lewis had become established as a champion among American evangelicals. Even stricter fundamentalists who normally disparaged the intellectual mainstream nonetheless cited Lewis's academic prestige as evidence of the credibility of the faith. In 1969 Chad Walsh, speaking as a mainline Protestant with broader theological sensibilities, expressed chagrin at "the unabashed delight that some extreme fundamentalists took in his work; though he was certainly never a formal member of their fellowship, they seemed to issue him guest-privilege cards on an astonishing scale."[31]

One bit of evidence that Lewis had become fully accepted among mainstream evangelicals was that in 1969 the flagship magazine *Christianity Today* was offering to subscribers a volume titled *C. S. Lewis: Five Best Books in One Volume*.[32] *Christianity Today* editor Harold Lindsell provided a brief introduction. Lindsell was known for his insistence on the "inerrancy" of Scripture as an essential gatekeeping doctrine. With that issue no doubt in mind, he remarked that "Lewis is not infallible" and added that "if he were alive today he would probably admit to having changed some of his ideas for he was willing to learn."[33]

By this time Lewis's reputation seems to have transcended intraevangelical debates. Furthermore, there is little evidence that rank-and-file enthusiasm was much shaped one way or another by what by the end of the 1970s could be described as "the growing flood of secondary literature" on Lewis.[34] In fact, the influence was largely the other way around. Lewis's grassroots popularity, which accelerated conspicuously in that decade, helped generate more books and studies. Even though the story of the reception of *Mere Christianity* has to be told largely through what has been published, it is more truly a myriad of stories, mostly unrecorded, of how the book was used and shared locally.

# Many-Sided *Mere Christianity*

Much of the growing popularity of *Mere Christianity* had to do with the individuals whose lives were changed by it. One person whose faith with initiated or renewed by the book would share that enthusiasm with friends, some of whom would similarly find it helpful and recommend or give it to his or her friends, so that its sales grew geometrically, as in a pyramid scheme. Many who were given the book might not read it, and many who read it would not find it helpful. Yet enough received it with enthusiasm that the word-of-mouth advertising and accelerating sales continued. Countless church groups have studied the book in settings where the enthusiasm of a few has been contagious. Church-related colleges and high schools often assigned it. In 1982 *Publisher's Weekly* reported that since 1963 some 1.62 million copies had been sold in the United States just as a trade paperback, thus putting it in the top twenty of all American books in that format, slightly ahead of *The Screwtape Letters*, of which 1.5 million copies had been sold. Both books also appeared in a number of other formats, in Lewis collections and British editions, and in translations that would have accounted for many more sales.[1]

The paradigmatic *Mere Christianity* conversion story was that of Chuck Colson. As special counsel to the U.S. president, Colson had been known as Richard Nixon's "hatchet man."[2] Colson was one of the leading figures implicated in the Watergate scandals that would end Nixon's presidency. As his life was falling apart in the summer of 1973, he turned to his friend Tom Phillips, chairman of the board of the Raytheon Corporation. Phillips had been converted a few years earlier at a Billy Graham crusade and had offered support. When Colson visited Phillips's home outside of Boston on a muggy summer evening, the two men sat on the front porch sipping tea. Philips urged Colson to "accept Christ." Colson was intrigued but wary. Toward the end of the evening Phillips handed him a copy of *Mere Christianity*. Phillips suggested that Colson read it on his upcoming vacation but asked if he could read him just one chapter. It was the chapter from *Christian Behaviour* titled "The Great Sin." "There is one vice," Lewis began, "of which no man in the world is free; which every one loathes when he sees it in someone else, and of which hardly any people, except Christians, ever imagine that they are guilty of themselves." Lewis said he knew people who readily admitted other vices but "I do not think I have ever heard anyone who was not a Christian accuse himself of this vice. . . . There is no fault . . . which we are more unconscious of in ourselves. And the more we have it ourselves, the more we dislike it in others." The vice that Lewis was talking about was "Pride or Self-Conceit." He went on to point out how pride "has been the chief cause of misery in every nation and family since the world began." These words, Colson later reported, "seemed to pound straight at me." And when Phillips got to Lewis's comment that "Pride is a spiritual cancer: it eats up the very possibility of love, or contentment, or even common sense," Colson saw it as summing up all that had gone on in the White House.[3]

Colson left that night on the edge of being converted, but he still had many lawyer-type questions to think through. During the succeeding days at a cottage in Maine he pored over *Mere Christianity*. He was especially impressed by what he came to describe as "the central thesis of Lewis's book and the essence of Christianity, . . . summed up in one mind-boggling sentence: *Jesus Christ is God*." As Lewis had said, if Jesus was not God, he was "a raving lunatic" to claim that he was God. And in that case Jesus would certainly not be "a great moral teacher." Lewis had helped make Colson see the astonishing implications for himself if Jesus's claim was true. He needed to make Jesus the "Lord of my life." After wrestling with the issues for several days, Colson finally offered a classic evangelical prayer of commitment: "Lord Jesus, I believe You. I accept you. Please come into my life. I commit it to You."[4]

The next year, 1974, Colson was indicted for obstruction of justice, pleaded guilty to some of the charges, and then served seven months in prison. He later would become a leading champion of prison ministry and prison reform. Colson had many book offers, but after his release from prison he chose an evangelical publisher for his autobiographical account centering on his conversion, titled *Born Again*. The timing could not have been better. The book's release in late February of 1976 coincided almost exactly with the dramatic emergence of dark-horse Democratic presidential candidate Jimmy Carter, who identified himself as being "born again." That sent reporters scurrying to find out the meaning of this phrase, previously unfamiliar to many of them, and to understand the massive American "evangelical" movement that had been largely ignored until it was recognized for its political potential. Just before the November election, *Newsweek* emblazoned its cover with "BORN AGAIN: The Evangelicals." The magazine tagged 1976 as "The Year of the Evangelicals."[5] In the meantime Colson's book had sold more than five hundred thousand copies, and a print run of two million had gone out to bookstores. By the end of the year it had been translated into eleven languages.[6] So Lewis and *Mere Christianity*, standing as they did near the center of the Colson conversion story, caught a wave of international publicity that reinforced the volume's standing as the book to give someone who might be open to seeking Christian faith.

Colson's conversion story was unusual in the drama of his situation and in the publicity that it elicited, but it would be easy to compile many comparable stories. In fact, the Wade Center at Wheaton did just that in two surveys, in 1986 and 1996. Many of the responses, rather than being strictly conversion accounts, tell of the respondents' struggling with a Christian upbringing or a narrow church and how Lewis, often through *Mere Christianity*, as one woman put it, "answered so many questions for me and cleared so many issues. My relationship with God has become *new* through Lewis—brighter—more vivid—more real." A man working as a missionary to university students in Germany wrote that "although I had been a believer from childhood, it was after reading *Mere Christianity* that I first became enthusiastic about my faith. If a man of Lewis's intellect can believe in God and in the redemptive work of Christ, then I have nothing to be ashamed of! And it grew from there."[7] For those more dramatically converted, *Mere Christianity* seems most often to have played the leading role among Lewis's works. To cite just one striking testimony, in a 1983 interview British evangelist Stephen F. Olford made the remarkable claim that he himself knew "not just scores, but hundreds of intellectual people . . . [who] have come to Christ subsequent to reading [*Mere Christianity*].[8] Such an estimate, based on just one highly respected man's observations, suggests how common the sort of experience Colson recorded seems to have been.

Celebrity conversions have continued to enhance the book's reputation. Perhaps the best known since Colson's time is that of the eminent scientist Francis

Collins, who served as the head of the Human Genome Project and later as the director of the National Institutes of Health. Collins tells of how as an atheistic young scientist he felt compelled to investigate the rational basis for his atheism. Eventually he brought his questions regarding Christianity to a local Methodist minister who gave him a copy of *Mere Christianity*. Collins writes that as he read Lewis during the next few days "I realized that all of my own constructs against the plausibility of the faith were those of a schoolboy. . . . Lewis seemed to know all of my objections, sometimes even before I had quite formulated them." When Collins later learned that "Lewis had himself been an atheist, who had set out to disprove faith on the basis of logical argument, I recognized how he could be so insightful about my path. It had been his path as well."[9] In 2006 Collins offered his own apologetic book, *The Language of God: A Scientist Presents Evidence for Belief*, which reached the bestseller lists. Collins recapitulated some of Lewis's arguments but added many others drawn from natural science.

Many of the most influential leaders of the British and American evangelical communities have been deeply shaped not just by *Mere Christianity* but by encounters with the whole corpus of Lewis's work. One of the earliest and best known of such cases was that of J. I. Packer, recounted in the preceding chapter. In these instances, the most characteristic story is not one of conversion from atheism but rather of discovering

Lewis as a young Christian, being greatly helped by him and profoundly influenced by his example.

In the twenty-first century several other of the most influential evangelical apologists were similarly influenced by Lewis as young Christians and see themselves as carrying on Lewis's work. One instance is that of N. T. Wright, the highly influential British New Testament scholar and prolific writer, who speaks of his "enormous admiration for Lewis, who I read in my teens and twenties voraciously. I read some passages so many times that I can recite them by heart."[10] Wright offers some substantial criticisms of *Mere Christianity*, especially in the area of Wright's own scholarly expertise, New Testament interpretation. Yet he remains deeply sympathetic and approaches his own work as an extension of that of Lewis, whose writings guided him in his early years. In 2006 Wright published his own introductory apologetic, *Simply Christian*, in which he "pays homage" to Lewis "by beginning with a similar but not identical argument about justice,"[11] but tries to build on, expand, and improve on Lewis for the twenty-first century.

Timothy Keller, founding pastor of Redeemer Presbyterian Church in New York City and another prolific and influential contemporary Christian apologist, likewise tells of being deeply influenced by Lewis during his early years and, despite some criticisms, continuing to have a strong admiration for Lewis's apologetic skills. Nonetheless, Keller found that *Mere Christianity* was not always as accessible to sophisticated New Yorkers as it might be. So he wrote his own basic apologetic work, *The Reason for God*, which starts by answering the most common contemporary objections to traditional Christianity and in some ways attempts to go beyond Lewis. Keller frequently quotes Lewis and sees his own successful work as a tribute to the don, whom he still regards as peerless. "My book," he says deferentially, "is *Mere Christianity for Dummies*.[12]

Alister McGrath is another widely influential author who has carried on Lewis's mission. Like Lewis, he grew up in Northern Ireland and as a young man was a militant atheist. After his conversion to Christianity in 1971, he discovered Lewis's work. Eventually he held some prominent professorships in theology at Oxford and became one of Britain's leading Christian apologists. Much of his work was influenced by Lewis. He has written a major biography of Lewis and also published a volume of insightful essays, *The Intellectual World of C. S. Lewis*.[13] Like other apologists who undertook to continue Lewis's work, McGrath has offered criticisms along with appreciation and seen one of his tasks as that of updating Lewis for the twenty-first century. McGrath has, for instance, published a handbook for Christian apologists, *Mere Apologetics: How to Help Seekers and Skeptics Find Faith*. As the title suggests, "The book's approach mirrors that of C. S. Lewis," and one can find aspects of *Mere Christianity* duly translated for twenty-first-century audiences.[14]

The people whose stories have been described are just some of the best-known and most influential figures in the British and American evangelical communities whose own careers have been shaped by reading Lewis, always including *Mere Christianity*. In one survey of about sixty evangelical leaders, twenty mentioned Lewis's books as the most influential on their lives, and eight specified *Mere Christianity*.[15] Early in the twenty-first century, sociologist D. Michael Lindsay interviewed 157 of the most influential evangelicals among American elites in politics, academia, the arts, and business. Lindsay reports that "nearly one in four of the people I interviewed mentioned Lewis' influence on their own spiritual journey, and may have read his works multiple times. One CEO told me, "I've read *Mere Christianity* six times . . . I almost have it memorized."[16]

In 2013, during the American "March Madness" collegiate basketball tournament, the Emerging Scholars Network of InterVarsity Christian Fellowship ran "The Best Christian Book of All Time Tournament." Beginning with sixty-four entries, participants voted for one in each of a series of paired competitors through elimination rounds. *Mere Christianity*, a first seed, easily got into the "Elite Eight," where it handily defeated Augustine's *City of God*. Then in the "Final Four" it beat Dietrich Bonhoeffer's *Cost of Discipleship*, but in the finals it was edged out by Augustine's *Confessions*.[17]

Although the emergence of *Mere Christianity* as one of the most revered of all texts among American evangelicals is the most remarkable story in the book's public life, that does not at all imply that it became exclusively identified with that segment of Christendom. For one thing, the book's strongly nonsectarian message runs counter to any such identification. For another, one can find comparable stories of its reception in other Christian communions, including broader Protestant denominations, and especially among Roman Catholics. One difference is that much of American evangelicalism has tended to neglect history and tradition in favor of getting directly back to the Bible and personal experience, so in such communities Lewis has filled a gap by offering a connection with an older and intellectually strong Christian heritage. For persons raised in communions with deeper institutional roots, such as confessional Protestants, Anglicans and their world affiliates, or adherents of the Eastern Orthodox and Roman Catholic faiths, *Mere Christianity* may also be popular as an evangelistic tool. But it is also more clearly subordinated to theologies and practices already firmly shaped by longstanding historical traditions.

Roman Catholics can point to their own lists of converts deeply influenced by Lewis. In the cases of many of these, Lewis not only helped shape their early faith but was instrumental in starting them on the road to Rome. That might seem paradoxical because Lewis was a Protestant from Northern Ireland and, as Tolkien and others have remarked, that heritage left him with an indelible prejudice against "papists" and with little attraction to the Roman Catholic Church as such. Nonetheless, as one Catholic champion of Lewis argues, "Many of the core beliefs he embraced as a 'mere Christian' placed him decidedly on the Catholic end of the theological spectrum."[18] Lewis was open to some Catholic beliefs and practices, such as Purgatory and having a confessor. But, more important, especially for people whose Christian experience had been shaped by a narrow sectarian Protestantism, one of the most refreshing things about discovering "mere Christianity" was to think of the faith in terms of its perennial qualities. That, in turn, could lead them toward Rome.

Catholic lists of converts influenced by Lewis include many who are well known. These include the famed RAF World War II hero and champion of the disabled Leonard Cheshire, the German economist E. F. Schumacher, and American writer Sheldon Vanauken, whose acclaimed *A Severe Mercy* recounts Lewis's profound personal influence on him in dealing with his wife's early death.[19] Novelist Walker Percy wrote in 1987, in his foreword to a book collecting stories of Catholic converts, that although, as would be expected, writers such as Thomas Aquinas or Thomas Merton are mentioned in the book as influences, "guess who turns up most often—C. S. Lewis! who, if he didn't make it all the way [to the Catholic Church], certainly handed over a goodly crew."[20] As *New York Times* columnist Ross Douthat explained elsewhere, "You start reading C. S. Lewis, then you're reading

G. K. Chesterton, then you're a Catholic. I knew a lot of people who did that in their 20s—I just did it earlier."[21]

As in the evangelical case, Catholic converts include some influential lay celebrities. One of the best known is Thomas S. Monaghan, founder of Domino's Pizza. Although already a practicing Catholic and a supporter of conservative Catholic causes, Monaghan in 1989 found his life profoundly changed by the same passage of "The Great Sin" in *Mere Christianity* that had led to Chuck Colson's conversion. So convinced was he of the evil of his own pride that he took what he described as "a millionaire's vow of poverty," divesting himself of some of his most prized possessions. These included ownership of the Detroit Tigers and a lavish Frank Lloyd Wright–style "dream house" that he left unfinished. Rather than seeking new self-aggrandizing competitive conquests, he devoted his energies to serving conservative Catholic education and other conservative causes.[22]

As was also true among evangelicals, a number of the most prominent Catholics whose faith was deeply shaped by Lewis dedicated themselves to carrying on his apologetic task. Not incidentally, most of these started out as evangelical or conservative Protestants for whom Lewis's perennial Christianity became a first step on the road to Rome. Among the earliest of these was Peter Kreeft, who, as a Christian Reformed student in the 1950s, discovered Lewis at Calvin College. Soon afterward he was led by reading Catholic authors to convert to Catholicism. He studied philosophy at Fordham and taught for many years at Boston College. One commentator refers to him as "perhaps the most lucid and prolific Catholic apologist in the English-speaking world."[23] Kreeft's efforts to emulate Lewis are evident in many of his works. In his *C. S. Lewis: A Critical Essay* he makes his exposition of Lewis's "mere Christianity" the central point of his argument. And memorably, in *Between Heaven & Hell* Kreeft creates a dialogue among John F. Kennedy, C. S. Lewis, and Aldous Huxley, who are imagined to be waiting together in a sort of limbo just after each had died on November 22, 1963. The centerpiece of the discussion is Lewis's successful defense of his "trilemma," often popularly represented as the proposition that Jesus was either Lord, lunatic, or liar, from *Mere Christianity*.

A number of other prominent writers, from evangelical backgrounds, first took up Lewis's tasks and eventually turned to Rome. The best known of these was Thomas Howard, who came from a well-known evangelical family and was the brother of the famous missionary and writer Elisabeth Elliot. Howard found Lewis under the tutelage of Clyde Kilby at Wheaton College in the 1950s and, like Lewis and Kilby, took up a career in literature. Soon after college Howard followed Lewis into the Episcopal Church, but in the 1980s he turned to Rome. His many books advocating Christian faith and Catholicism reflect themes drawn from Lewis.[24] A similar story is that of Dwight D. Longenecker, who discovered Lewis while a student in the 1970s at Bob Jones University, a militantly anti-Catholic fundamentalist stronghold in South Carolina. Longenecker tells of finding what Lewis called "mere Christianity" to be a bridge between the biblicist faith in which he had been reared and the true roots of that faith in a more substantial European tradition. Longenecker eventually converted to Catholicism, entered the priesthood, and is known for many books expounding the faith.[25] Francis Beckwith, another prolific defender of Christianity who acknowledges a large debt to Lewis, converted to Roman Catholicism in 2007 near the end of his term as president of the Evangelical Theological Society.[26]

Among readers of Lewis the most familiar name in the ranks of former evangelical converts to Catholicism is Walter Hooper. From North Carolina, Hooper had become a Christian in the mid-1950s, helped by reading Lewis, and after some years of correspondence he came to serve as Lewis's personal secretary in 1963. After Lewis's death Hooper dedicated himself to promoting Lewis's works and legacy. He became the literary adviser to the estate of C. S. Lewis and edited many of Lewis's previously unpublished works, as well as writing much about Lewis himself. In 1984 Hooper had an audience with Pope John Paul II, whom he already greatly revered. Hooper found the Pope to be a well-acquainted admirer of Lewis and learned that he had promoted Lewis's works while the bishop of Krakow. In 1988 Hooper was received into the Roman Catholic Church.[27]

Some of the Roman Catholic admirers of Lewis nonetheless sharply criticize the preface to *Mere Christianity*, in which, as noted in chapter 4, he likens "mere Christianity" to a hall that leads to many rooms. Lewis states, "The hall is a place to wait in, a place from which to try the various doors, not a place to live in." So he urges readers to choose particular rooms for themselves and then to be generous to those who have made other choices. Christopher Derrick, for instance, in his 1981 book *C. S. Lewis and the Church of Rome*, responded, "This preface comes close to being an ecumenical manifesto and has been taken as such by many." Yet "it is, in fact," Derrick explains, "a specifically (though often unconsciously) Protestant understanding of the relationship between Christianity and the Churches. It implies a clear-cut rejection of the Catholic view." So although Derrick affirms, "I take *Mere Christianity* to be a wise, important, and useful book," he also declares that "its attempt to be ecumenical is self-defeating."[28] Ian Kerr, who acknowledges that *Mere Christianity* was an "enormous influence" on him in his teens, argues along similar lines: "The Roman Catholic Church would have to insist that the envisaged house *is* the Roman Catholic Church, with the other communions as more or less attached to it as annexes or outbuildings." So, Kerr concludes, "The whole concept of a common hall with different rooms opening off it is not an acceptable ecclesiastical model from the Catholic point of view."[29] Father Dwight D. Longenecker agrees with such criticisms in his expositions of Lewis and argues that the corrective to Lewis's limited vision in *Mere Christianity* is, as the title of a Longenecker book puts it, *More Christianity*.[30]

Lewis is popular in many other Christian communions and denominations. In 1990 Andrew Walker, the director of the C. S. Lewis Centre for the Study of Religion and Modernity in London and a lay theologian in the Eastern Orthodox tradition, described Lewis as "avidly read and admired by thousands of people in the Eastern churches." Kallistos Ware, an English bishop within the Eastern Orthodox Church, similarly affirmed that "Lewis has an enthusiastic following among Orthodox Christians" and that "there are Orthodox bookshops which stock virtually no works by any non-Orthodox author, with one striking exception—C. S. Lewis." Ware adds that he can "think of Orthodox clergy, strictly traditionalist in their outlook, who use *Mere Christianity* as their main textbook when instructing catechumens."[31] Ware himself argues that there are so many points of harmony between Lewis's outlook and Orthodox theology that Lewis "has a strong claim to be considered an 'anonymous Orthodox.'" Much as many Catholic interpreters can see Lewis as almost on the road to Rome, Orthodox Christians can view him as virtually one of their own.[32]

Evangelical historian Mark Noll has reflected on a significant dimension of "mere Christianity" that is also difficult to measure. "The phrase 'mere Christianity,'" he observes, "has become a widely used code to designate a meaningful body of belief that unites moderate to conservative Christians from all denominations." Writing at the end of the twentieth century, Noll noted the remarkable degree of practical Christian ecumenicity that had developed since midcentury. That ecumenicity was not institutional but rather reflected a growing sense among Christians of many communions worldwide with which they shared the most essential elements of the faith of Christians through the ages. For instance, Christians of many church affiliations might readily engage in common projects of scholarship, charity, or social reform with a sense of practical unity that "mere Christianity" aptly described.[33] So, even though there is resistance, among Catholics and others, to allowing the appeal to shared "mere Christianity" to substitute for church traditions of doctrine and worship,[34] the concept has taken on a life of its own as a way of expressing unity among moderate and conservative believers despite their differing ecclesiastical ties.[35]

Lewis and *Mere Christianity* even have a considerable following among Mormons. Richard Ostling, former religion editor at *Time* and co-author of the 1999 volume *Mormon America*, reports that one of the surprises was "the extraordinary interest in C. S. Lewis among Mormons and the belief that Lewis was almost a crypto-Mormon."[36] Despite acknowledged differences between Lewis's classic orthodoxy and Latter-day Saints theology, Mormons can find more in common than not with Lewis's experiential accounts of what it means to embrace Christ, of the nature of human sinfulness, of pride as "the Great Sin," and of giving up self and finding Christ.[37] Mormon theologian Robert Millet was a principal organizer of a conference at Brigham Young University in 1998 honoring the centenary of Lewis birth. According to Millet, who also spoke on Lewis from a Mormon perspective at a similar event at Wheaton College that same year, "In his adherence to 'mere Christianity,' he is everyman's preacher, every woman's exegete. He is the thinking Christian's supreme apologist."[38]

Various C. S. Lewis societies have contributed to promoting Lewis's work and in bringing together admirers of Lewis from varieties of denominations. Not surprisingly, most of these are in the United States. The first was the New York C. S. Lewis Society, established in 1969. Since then the group has published its own journal and sponsored many speakers and gatherings on Lewis and related topics. By the end of the twentieth century there were more than a dozen Lewis societies or institutes, not only in the United States but also in Great Britain and Canada, and even one in Japan.[39] One of the largest and most active groups has been the C. S. Lewis Foundation, a California-based organization that has since the late 1980s sponsored C. S. Lewis summer institutes in England, offering lectures from impressive lineups of Lewis scholars and admirers. The Foundation also has purchased the Lewis home, the Kilns, and maintains it as a study center that is also open for tours.

*Mere Christianity* has been translated into at least thirty-six languages and so has been a presence in many parts of the world. Yet, like the "life" of the book among the vast majority of English-speakers who have encountered it, the stories of the use of the book in other places remain almost entirely unrecorded.[40] The only parts of the world where it appears to have had an impact beyond that of ordinary readership are the former Communist lands of Eastern Europe and China. In both places *Mere Christianity* seems to have played a role as a handbook for reintroducing (or introducing) people to Christianity.

Very soon after the breakup of the Soviet empire, *Mere Christianity* was published in Albanian, Bulgarian, Croatian, Czech, Estonian, Hungarian, Lithuanian, Romanian, Russian, Slovakian, and Slovene. The book has been a resource, including in Orthodox circles, in rebuilding Christian influences. Even before the fall of the Soviet Union, some evangelical groups were reportedly smuggling into East Germany copies of *Pardon, ich bin Christ: Meine Argumente für den Glauben*, the German version of *Mere Christianity*, which they found to be in considerable demand. In one instance these were discovered along with a supply of Bibles by East German officials who confiscated Lewis's work as presumably subversive.[41] During the Communist era the first part of the book was published in Czech under the title *Hovory* (Talks). Called simply the "blue book," this unauthorized version, distributed from a Christian worker's basement, reportedly had a significant impact, especially in presenting Christianity to intellectuals.[42]

The most remarkable world story is from China. According to one veteran American teacher, *Mere Christianity* is the book, next to the Bible, that Chinese intellectual Christians are most likely to have read. That report is confirmed by the sales of a recent Chinese translation, which, since its publication in 2007, had sold sixty thousand copies by 2014. One source of that interest has been the influence of the prestigious Chinese intellectual Guanghu He. Professor He, who studied in the United States, is reported to have said that the place of C. S. Lewis in the English-speaking world is comparable to that of Lu Xun, the early twentieth-century novelist, critic, and essayist, in the Chinese-speaking world. Professor He has written prefaces for publications of Lewis's works and trained doctoral and other students, including translators of *Mere Christianity*, in studies of Lewis. According to a selection from some three thousand online comments about the Chinese version of *Mere Christianity*, its use and impact are strikingly similar to what one finds in the United States. Quite a few report that they have bought ten or twenty copies to give to their friends. Many say that it "played a decisive role in my conversion" or it "totally changed my view of Christianity" or it "dispelled the last tinge of my doubt about Christianity." One writes, "I marvel at Lewis's wisdom—with a few words he makes the proposition that Jesus is not God collapse, and I can find no fault with his argument. Lewis presents a pure, ecumenical Christianity, free from any theological or political dissension." Another writes privately, "I consider *Mere Christianity* to be the one book that enlightened me in a way that opens the possibility of reason being in harmony with faith. In fact, it also shows how reason by itself is not sufficient: it only gets you so far. After that you have to let faith carry you."[43]

Still, the most important story regarding *Mere Christianity* is that of its extensive impact in the United States. By far the majority of the books about Lewis and his apologetics have been by Americans. As many have observed, Lewis the Oxford don seems to carry an unusual aura of authority for many Americans. That authority may be strongest in communities that do not have strong intellectual traditions of their own. Stephanie Derrick, in comparing the British and American receptions of Lewis, points out that Lewis has less often been treated with such reverence in Great Britain. There, Lewis was long a more controversial figure. Furthermore, because church practice in the United Kingdom declined far more rapidly than in the United States in the later twentieth century, Lewis had a smaller number of devoted followers in his homeland. Derrick also observes that regard for Lewis may be making a comeback in Britain since the beginning of the twenty-first century. She quotes a remark from Christopher Hitchens in his 2007 book *God Is Not Great* that Lewis has "recently reemerged as the most popular Christian apologist" and is the "main chosen propaganda vehicle for Christianity in our time."[44] Whether hated or loved, Lewis seems now, more than a generation ago, to be taken seriously in his own country.

Contrary to his expectations that his works would soon be forgotten, Lewis is far better known in the twenty-first century than he was at the time of his death in 1963. He is most famous as the author of the *Chronicles of Narnia*, and that reputation is enhanced by his close association with J.R.R. Tolkien, whose *Hobbit* and *Lord of the Rings* have become even more immensely successful since the 1960s. Lewis also reached a certain level of stardom by being portrayed by Anthony Hopkins in a major 1993 motion picture, *Shadowlands*, which is based on an earlier BBC film and successful stage play of the same name dramatizing his relationship with and marriage to Joy Davidman and her death. Even though Lewis is depicted there as somewhat naïve as an apologist, he is also presented as a major historical figure of depth and complexity. Further heightening Lewis's fame have been the tremendously successful Narnia films, the first three of which appeared in 2005, 2008, and 2010 and are said to have grossed over $1.5 billion worldwide among them.[45]

Lewis was a multifaceted figure, and his various sorts of fame have reinforced each other. On November 22, 2013, on the fiftieth anniversary of his death, he received the ultimate British recognition with the dedication of a memorial stone in Westminster Abbey to "C. S. Lewis, Writer, Scholar, Apologist." Even if during his lifetime his popular apologetics had been divisive and cost him some of his reputation among his peers, it was now recognized as one of his lasting achievements. Among the presentations made in the dedication service was the playing of an excerpt from the sole surviving recording of his BBC broadcast from "Beyond Personality."[46]

# Critigues

Wherever *Mere Christianity* has been read, it has been hated as well as loved. Nonetheless, as a popular presentation of the faith it has drawn less systematic criticism than would a book that purported to be a definitive treatise on Christian apologetics and theology. Literary scholar Margaret P. Hannay summarized the mix of attitudes well in 1981, noting that Lewis's *Mere Christianity* is "the most popular and the most disparaged of his works, probably because its fans have spoken of it as a profound piece of theology, while it is, as was designed to be, only a primer." Hannay adds that "anyone ignorant of Christian doctrine can learn much from it, but anyone seriously interested in theology must go beyond it, reading both Lewis's sources, the patristic writers like St. Augustine and St. Athanasius, and more contemporary theologians. But the very simplicity of *Mere Christianity* makes it likely to endure."[1]

The one prominent and sustained attack on Lewis's thought in which *Mere Christianity* plays more than an incidental role is that by John Beversluis. As did Peter Kreeft, Beversluis graduated from Calvin College in the 1950s and went on to study philosophy, but in his case he turned away from any traditional faith. In 1985 he published *C. S. Lewis and the Search for Rational Religion*, and then in 2007 he offered a thoroughly "revised and updated" edition in which he carefully responded to his often irate critics. In this second edition he remarked that he had expected criticism, but not "the *kind* of criticism" that he had received. Although some reviewers of the first edition were convinced by his arguments, the many defenders of Lewis denounced them as "'facile,' 'shallow,' 'based on misunderstandings,' 'unfair,' 'underhanded,' 'intellectually dishonest,' and even despicable.'"[2] Beversluis attributed these harsh dismissals to the reverence in which Lewis is held by his fans and scholarly protectors, and he offered his reasoned responses to the substance of original critiques.[3]

Beversluis's point of departure is Lewis's remark in *Mere Christianity* "I am not asking anyone to accept Christianity if his best reasoning tells him that the weight of evidence is against it."[4] Beversluis takes this to mean that "according to Lewis, . . . the question of whether or not to become a Christian is a matter of sorting out and examining the evidence."[5] Beversluis accordingly translates each of Lewis's main arguments into propositions, analyzes their logic, and concludes that each is built on faulty reasoning and hence that Lewis's "case for Christianity" fails. Typically, says

Beversluis, "the apparent cogency of his [Lewis's] arguments depends on his rhetoric rather than his logic." Lewis, he says, is a brilliant rhetorician who most typically makes arguments look compelling by offering false choices. He presents two (or perhaps three) possibilities for explaining a phenomenon. He then purports to refute one (or two) of these, thus leaving the traditional Christian view as the only one still standing. He uses sleight of hand by representing the alternatives to Christianity in caricatured or incomplete "straw men" forms that can easily be dismissed, when in fact there are stronger versions of the alternatives that can convincingly explain the phenomena.[6] "My complaint about the Broadcast Talks," says Beversluis, "is not that Lewis fails to be as thorough as his subject matter demands, but that he gives the impression of being thorough."[7]

Beversluis deals with the whole corpus of Lewis's apologetic works, but two of his major points figure prominently in *Mere Christianity*.[8] The first is Lewis's opening pre-evangelistic argument that our conviction that there must be a real right and wrong is best explained as the product of a higher being who established that law rather than as a product of "herd instinct" or "mere social convention." Beversluis argues, to the contrary, that our moral beliefs can be "much more plausibly" explained as "rules developed over thousands of years whose purpose is to minimize human suffering and to promote human flourishing." So the strength of our convictions about the reality of right and wrong only illustrates "how deeply we participate in the moral life and practices of the society that gave us life and our very moral identity."[9] Another conspicuous flaw for Beversluis is Lewis's use in book 2 of *Mere Christianity* of the famous "trilemma." Beversluis argues that there are perfectly good alternatives to "liar or lunatic" that have just as much credibility as that Jesus was actually God incarnate. For instance, Jesus's disciples might have misinterpreted his claims in the later biblical accounts. Or Jesus might have been suffering from mental illness and delusions, despite his great moral teaching.[10]

Of the many responses to Beversluis, the most thorough of the strictly philosophical replies is Victor Reppert's in *C. S. Lewis's Dangerous Idea: In Defense of the Argument from Reason*.[11] Reppert defends Lewis's arguments, contending that Lewis does not set up straw men in order to knock down atheistic alternatives but rather shows the absurdities that follow from actual positions that atheists affirm. Nonetheless, says Reppert, Lewis is not claiming that the arguments for Christianity are so decisive that they will compel all people or that atheists can be accused of being irrational for not assenting. Rather, despite Lewis's sometimes triumphalist tone when dismissing theistic alternatives, Reppert describes Lewis as what philosophers call "a critical rationalist" who recognizes that, as Lewis himself put it, "there is evidence both for and against the Christian propositions which fully rational minds, working honestly, can assess differently."[12]

Reppert's observations reflect a broad consensus found among most interpreters regarding the role of reason in Lewis's apologetics. According to this consensus, critics such as Beversluis are correct in pointing out that many of Lewis's arguments are not strictly logical demonstrations,[13] but they err in overestimating the degree to which Lewis rested his case for Christianity on reason alone. Lewis was not simply on a "search for rational religion," as Beversluis's title suggests. Lewis did think that Christian belief could be shown to be consistent with the best reasoning, but, as his own spiritual biography makes clear, he also believed that the case for Christianity rested on far more than reason alone. Michael Ward makes this point well in an analysis of the essential interrelationship of imagination and reason in Lewis's own life and in his apologetics. In a 1939 essay Lewis spoke of imagination as "the organ of meaning" and reason as "the natural organ of truth."[14] So reason cannot operate independent of the imagination that shapes meaning. Accordingly, says Ward, what was standing in the way of Lewis's conversion to Christianity, and hence what brought him to conversion, was not his reason but his imagination. In his life-changing late-night walk with his close friends J.R.R. Tolkien and Hugo Dyson, he came to see the Incarnation, Crucifixion, and Resurrection of Christ as "true myth," that is, as earth-shaking and transformative of historical realities. As Lewis wrote to his friend and confidant Arthur Greeves, "What has been holding me back . . . has not been so much a difficulty in believing as a difficulty in knowing what the doctrine *meant*." [15] Reason is also necessary to belief in that beliefs cannot be contrary to reason. But reason by itself cannot be expected to compel assent.[16]

So, according to Ward and many others (as I recount in my concluding chapter), Lewis in his apologetics is not naïvely appealing to universal reason as the basis for faith[17] but rather to the whole person. Lewis did have a high regard for reasoning that could appeal to something like the common sense of humankind, based on commonalities of human experience. So he believed that reasoned arguments might be persuasive to many people, even if they would not be universally compelling to all candid thinkers. But the common sense of humankind involved not only reason but also moral sensibilities, affections, imagination, will, and emotions, all of which were inextricably intertwined.

One implication for those who regard Lewis as seeing reason as so inextricably embedded with these other dimensions of the whole person is that they see his use of rhetoric as one of the great virtues of his apologetics rather than as a sleight-of-hand device, as critics like Beversluis would have it. Rhetoric, metaphor, and analogy serve to excite the imagination of his audience. As Ward puts it, compared to otherwise similar works of apologetics, *Mere Christianity* "stands out for the wealth of imagery it employs." In such a view, imagery is not incidental to Lewis's reasoned arguments but is integral to them. His "apologetic language benefits from being vivid, sensory, and chosen with poetic, not just abstractly rational, intent."[18]

As should already be apparent, the argument in *Mere Christianity* that both has been the most celebrated and also has received by far the most negative responses is the so-called trilemma that Lewis sketches in book 2: that one cannot accept Jesus as just a great moral teacher who was not God; either Jesus was correct in his astonishing claim to be God or he was an evil self-aggrandizing liar or he was a lunatic. This argument has become closely associated with Lewis, but it is far from original with him. Versions of it can be traced as far back as Augustine,[19] and it was often used in modern apologetics, including in an extended version by G. K. Chesterton in *The Everlasting Man*,[20] a volume that Lewis greatly admired. Lewis himself was aware that there was a fourth option: that the disciples might have invented the story that Jesus claimed to be God. In fact, according to the original script of his radio broadcast, Lewis actually addressed this objection: "The theory," he had said, "only saddles you with twelve lunatics instead of one."[21] Lewis dropped this remark for the publications, presumably thinking that its very brief and dismissive form might raise more questions than it answered.

Ever since Lewis's version of the trilemma first appeared in print, critics have questioned its validity. Most often they have raised the objection that Lewis had intended to head off with his remark about the "twelve lunatics." They typically point out that many modern biblical critics believe that the Gospels do not accurately represent what Jesus said or thought about himself but record only what his disciples and followers later claimed about him.[22] Some popularizations of this objection characterize the choice as "Lord, Liar, Lunatic, or *Legend*." Lewis himself did not have much patience with modern critical biblical scholarship, which he believed typically begged questions by starting with ruling out the miraculous and so inevitably concluding that biblical materials were best understood by whatever was the best naturalistic supposition.[23] In what became *Mere Christianity* Lewis was addressing a popular audience rather than scholars and so did not pursue the lengthy digression that answering such objections would have involved.

The other objection most often offered to the trilemma is that it is indeed possible that someone who was a great moral teacher might also have suffered from a mental illness or delusion that would have led him to believe that he was God.[24] Lewis responded to this objection with the observation that no other great moral teacher has ever been considered to be God. Furthermore, among a monotheistic Jewish audience, where "God" meant "the Being outside the universe who had made it and was infinitely different from anything else," such a claim would have been especially shocking. The magnitude of such a delusion would inevitably have undermined the person's whole mind.[25] Many critics remain unconvinced. It is easy, for instance, to find Web sites with headings such as "Atheism 101: How to Respond to the Lord, Liar, Lunatic Argument?"

Even some of Lewis's great admirers have questioned the cogency of the trilemma and some other of Lewis's arguments. New Testament scholar N. T. Wright is especially critical of the trilemma on the grounds that Lewis entirely neglected the Jewish Old Testament background of Jesus's time and so did not recognize the degree to which Jesus's claims to be the Son of God would have been understood through the already existent incarnational principles of Jewish temple worship. Wright also argues that a number of Lewis's doctrinal formulations are crude or fuzzy and that he simply omitted other crucial doctrines such as Christ's victory on the cross, the defeat of the Devil, and the meaning of Easter for the establishment of the Kingdom of God involving a social and political ethic. Wright declares that, "as another imperfect apologist, I salute a great master," but nonetheless he sees *Mere Christianity* as "a fine but leaky building."[26] Alister McGrath, who has provided both an insightful biography of Lewis and some of the most helpful analysis of his apologetics, notes that "it is easy to criticize *Mere Christianity* on account of its simple ideas," but that it has to be viewed for what it is as a popular book in which fine distinctions are sacrificed to readability. "*Mere Christianity*," says McGrath, "is an informal handshake to begin a more formal acquaintance and conversation. There is much more that needs to be said." Even so, McGrath singles out the trilemma as a particularly "weak argument" and observes that non-believers can easily think of alternatives to the choices offered.[27]

Despite all these criticisms, Lewis's trilemma has its serious philosophical defenders. David A. Horner has responded specifically to Beversluis's version of the critique in a volume titled *C. S. Lewis as Philosopher*, concluding that Lewis's point is still valid, that the Christian hypothesis "covers the facts" better than any other hypothesis.[28] And Donald T. Williams, another philosopher, has responded to a wider range of critics, including N. T. Wright.[29] Horner and Williams both make the point that Lewis is not addressing people sophisticated regarding issues of biblical interpretation; rather, he speaks to the sorts of readers who already say, "I'm ready to accept Jesus as a great moral teacher, but I don't accept his claim to be God." The argument has much greater force for those who already admire Jesus as a great teacher. Horner and Williams also argue that if Lewis's formulation in *Mere Christianity* is expanded it can be made to work even with more sophisticated audiences. Peter Kreeft, who does expand the argument at length in *Between Heaven and Hell*, is even more enthusiastic, calling it "the most important argument in Christian apologetics."[30]

Even if Lewis's trilemma may not be an airtight logical argument, it has proven to be one of the most popular and persuasive passages of *Mere Christianity* for its target audience: laypeople who may be open to the claims of Christianity. Although atheists are not likely to be persuaded by that or any other argument, for those open enough to be already listening to or reading Lewis it is an example of how Lewis persuades through a combination of reasoning and rhetoric that speaks to sentiments they already have. Chuck Colson is just one of many converts who have found the argument especially powerful. More recently the best-known re-formulation of the argument has come from U-2 lead singer Bono. Asked in an interview whether Jesus Christ's being the Son of God was a "farfetched idea," Bono responded that many people like to think of Jesus as a "great prophet," but when he started saying, "I am the Messiah" and "I am God incarnate," the reaction was different:

> At this point, everyone starts staring at their shoes and says, *Oh my God, he's gonna keep saying this.* So what you're left with is: either Christ was who He said. He was the Messiah or a complete nutcase. I mean, we're talking nutcase on the level of Charles Manson. . . . The idea that the entire course of civilization for over half the globe could have its fate turned upside-down by a nutcase, for me, *that's* far-fetched.[31]

The other major topic in *Mere Christianity* on which Lewis is most frequently criticized is his views on women and gender. After arguing in his chapter ti-tled "Christian Marriage" that vows ought to be per-manent and not subordinated to being "in love," Lewis turns to justifying the Christian marriage promise, then standard, that wives are to obey their husbands. First he argues that, just practically speaking, someone needs to have the last word. He then goes on with a bit of psychologizing as to why it should be the husband. Wives, he says, do not admire other households in which the women run things. Furthermore, men are naturally better at "foreign policy," or dealing with the outside world, than are women, who fight for their children with "intense family patriotism" and so are less likely to be just toward their neighbors.[32] And in his chapter "The Great Sin," on pride, he gratuitously throws in his view that the kind of pretty girl who will "spread misery wherever she goes by collecting admirers" is "quite often sexually frigid."[33]

Even in his own day, Lewis did not always get a pass for such remarks. Dorothy Sayers, for instance, wrote to one correspondent, "I do admit that he is apt to write shocking nonsense about women and marriage." And to another she said that she liked Lewis "very much, and [I] always find him stimulating and amusing. One just has to accept the fact that there is a complete blank in his mind where women are concerned."[34] As in Sayers's case, many women seem to have been ready to look beyond such offhand remarks by a bachelor, and the great majority of Lewis's correspondents were women.[35]

In recent times, since the prevailing views on women and gender have been revolutionized in much of the world, the consensus among Lewis's admirers is to be a bit embarrassed for Lewis. Alister McGrath, for instance, comments that they "make Lewis look very dated" and that "it must be recognized that Lewis's social and moral assumptions now pose a significant barrier to . . . [*Mere Christianity*'s] intended audience" of those outside the church.[36] Alan Jacobs, another admiring biographer, points out that because "mere Christianity" was meant to summarize "the belief that has been common to nearly all Christians at all times," Lewis did not think his views were controversial, as indeed the idea of male headship in marriage was standard fare among Christians in the 1940s. Lewis also took a stand, later in the 1940s, against the ordination of women, a matter that did involve controversy and on which he stood on the more conservative side. "Matters like this," observes Jacobs, "can be clarified, but beyond them Lewis's attitude toward women becomes difficult to understand much less to explain." Particularly, Jacobs has in mind "some extraordinarily silly things about women" that he says most notably in *Mere Christianity*.[37]

Lewis's remarks in *Mere Christianity*, especially because of their evidently offhand character, play only a minor role in a considerable literature regarding his views on gender. His correspondence, his fiction, his views on women's ordination, his actual relations with women, and his reflections on his marriage and the death of his wife, Joy, in *A Grief Observed*, provide much richer sources.[38] So far as the views expressed on these issues in *Mere Christianity* are concerned, analysis that goes beyond saying they are simply outdated and deplorable is well represented[39] in the most sustained recent study, Mary Stewart Van Leeuwen's *A Sword between the Sexes?: C. S. Lewis and the Gender Debates.* Van Leeuwen, an ardent Christian feminist who acknowledges an early personal debt to Lewis's writings, argues that his views on women and gender were in flux. In the 1940s he held hierarchical and essentialist views of relationships between men and women, but by his latter years, especially as he was influenced by Joy Davidman, he was moving toward viewing gendered relationships in more egalitarian ways and as shaped by changing social constructions.[40] Moreover, even though one can find remarks in his writings that can be seen as "misogynist," Lewis was a much "better man than his theories" as a mentor and a colleague to women.[41] So Van Leeuwen's point is that there is no reason to take Lewis's views in this area as normative. And one might suppose that had Lewis lived long enough, his views would have continued to evolve.

However off-putting Lewis's remarks on women and gender in *Mere Christianity* may be, they are also comments that most readers can recognize for what they are. They are observations that Lewis had reason to believe would resonate with much of his 1940s audience. For some in later times they may have been reasons to dismiss Lewis and the book, but most readers easily identify them as dated attitudes that can be passed over as wholly peripheral to Lewis's primary concerns with the central perennial teachings of the faith.

# The Lasting Vitality of *Mere Christianity*

C. S. Lewis was acutely aware of changing reading tastes and so had expected his works soon to go out of style. Even in the decades after his death, when his books instead grew in popularity, critics were predicting that the world was changing too fast for such appeal to long continue. Lyle Dorsett, who directed the Marion E. Wade Center at Wheaton College from 1983 to 1990, observed that during his time there an "endless throng of editors, critics, and scholars came through the doors predicting the end of Lewis's ability to speak to a new generation."[1] Since then, even though Lewis's popularity has not waned, such prophets can occasionally still be found who say that Lewis will not be able to communicate to upcoming postmodern generations.[2] Perhaps someday such predictions will prove true. But for now the question regarding *Mere Christianity* is this: Why has it not faded in the way almost every other nonfiction book of the 1940s and 1950s has?

Over the past several decades a host of commentators have offered answers to this question regarding the genius and the ongoing appeal of Lewis in *Mere Christianity*. It would be impossible to begin to summarize all of these. What follows is a distillation of the most compelling insights that represent a consensus of opinion.

## 1. Lewis looks for timeless truths as opposed to the culturally bound

Almost every sympathetic analyst of Lewis's apologetics has made this point in one way or another. Lewis's ability to direct his audiences toward the realities conveyed in the perennial Christian message is a manifestation of one of the most fundamental traits of his outlook: his conviction that ideas that have stood the test of time are more likely to be reliable than the latest fashionable views of one's own day.

This trait, in turn, developed from Lewis's own deeply felt experiences. As a young man he had been so enthralled by modern thought that he had become a deeply disillusioned atheist. Then, during years of searching, he came to recognize the passing and ephemeral character of modern dogmas. During his quest for truth as a young man at Oxford in the 1920s, he took to heart his friend Owen Barfield's observations regarding "chronological snobbery." Many of the most heralded "advances" in modern thought, he came to see, would appear to later generations to be quaintly naïve. As he explained in a later essay, he rejected the "Great Myth" that had captivated him in his younger days. That was the modern myth that regarded history as basically an evolutionary progression from earlier, more primitive times of relative ignorance toward the triumph of modern scientifically based illumination.[3]

As a literary scholar with immense learning about human thought and imagination from other eras, Lewis was eminently positioned to be a guide in sorting out the perennial from the time-bound. His works of literary criticism are exemplary in explaining how the assumptions of earlier ages differed from his own. Each time and place has characteristic insights from which we may learn but also blind spots and misleading mythologies. So, for instance, in Lewis's *English Literature in the Sixteenth Century, Excluding Drama* (1952), his contribution to *The Oxford History of English Literature*, he titled his introductory chapter "The New Learning and the New Ignorance," a title he might have assigned to twentieth-century thought as well.

Lewis offered one of his most memorable expositions of the value of the wisdom of the past in gaining a proper perspective of modern times in a lay sermon, "Learning in Wartime," that he preached in Oxford in September 1939. Britain and France had just declared war on Germany, and students were asking why they should study the ancients at a time when there were so many urgent present needs. Lewis's answer was that, rather than being impractical, learning from great writers of other eras was one of the needs of the hour. Especially in times of crisis, people need perspective from the past in order to recognize that "much which seems certain to the uneducated is merely temporary fashion." One "who has lived in many places is not likely to be deceived by the local errors of his native village; the scholar has lived in many times and is therefore in some degree immune from the great cataract of nonsense that pours from the press and the microphone of his own age."[4]

Lewis's literary excursions into many other times and places made him especially alert to the larger intellectual trends of the day that characterized contemporary culture, especially the reliance on scientific models. In his critiques of such outlooks he typically tried to acknowledge their practical accomplishments while questioning their unproven assumptions and claims to revolutionize understandings of the basic human condition. For instance, in *Christian Behaviour* he distinguished between the useful techniques of Freudian psychoanalysis and the naïvete of Freud as an amateur philosopher. Lewis often made a similar distinction between true science that produced much valuable knowledge and naïve naturalistic philosophies of scientism built around the unproven assumption that the scientific study of nature produces the highest form of knowledge. In Lewis's trilogy of interplanetary novels, *Out of the Silent Planet* (1938), *Perelandra* (1943), and *That Hideous Strength* (1945), the villains are pseudoscientists who have delusional visions of remaking the universe by using science to subdue nature. In *Screwtape*, the senior devil likewise promotes scientism. Screwtape warns his protégé, Wormwood, to keep his "patient" away from "real sciences" but to perhaps permit him to dabble in economics or sociology. "But the best of all is to let him read no science but to give him the general idea that he knows it all and that everything he happens to have picked up in casual talk and reading is 'the results of modern investigation.'"[5]

Lewis's preferences for timeless truths as opposed to the latest insights is a primary feature explaining the lasting vitality of *Mere Christianity*. In the mid–twentieth century academics and other sophisticates who prided themselves on being up to date might dismiss Lewis's viewpoints as antiquated. For instance, he had to suffer the scorn of some of his Oxford colleagues. Yet today it is twentieth-century philosophies and confident predications of a world guided by scientific understandings that seem quaint and sadly out of style. Most of contemporary thought is still based on naturalistic premises, but it is also riddled with the contradictions among modernist hopes and postmodern subversions of those hopes. And mid–twentieth century expert scientific advice for guiding one's life often looks naïve. Lewis's critiques of modernity and his warnings against being captivated by the spirit of the age or by its popular partisanships appear, in contrast, as prophetic. At least a fair number of readers find them so. And to the extent that Lewis succeeded in his quest to present perennial Christian truths, these have proved as compelling in our times as in his own.

An important corollary to Lewis's concentration on the perennial as opposed to the culturally bound is that Lewis avoids tying his presentation to controversial political or social issues of his day.[6] That was partly dictated by the constraints involved in addressing nationwide radio audiences during wartime. But it also reflected Lewis's disposition. He had little interest in politics and seldom read the newspapers. He was concerned, rather, with deeper cultural trends such as the philosophical movements he addressed in *The Abolition of Man*. Those trends did involve the practical matter of what was being taught in the schools. Such issues fit with his concerns related to preparation for evangelism. If some of the modern ideas took over the whole culture, that would further stultify people's natural moral sensibilities. Yet when it came to *Mere Christianity*, which involved evangelism as well as preevangelism, Lewis was careful to stay away from sociopolitical issues.

Lewis was quite explicit in avoiding the political temptation so prominent among Christians of his day and since. Screwtape recommends that Wormwood suggest that his patient's political views are part of his religion. "Then let him, under the influence of partisan spirit, come to regard it as the most important part." The final step is to have "the patient see his Christianity as valuable chiefly for the excellent arguments it provides for his party's positions."[7] Accordingly, Lewis himself was careful to avoid the snare of tying Christianity to partisan politics that has so often diverted people from the essence of the faith, especially in eras of participatory democracy.

Lewis has sometimes been criticized for making the Gospel too individualistic.[8] He was, nonetheless, clear about his priorities. If perennial Christianity was true, one's eternal relationship to God was the overwhelmingly preeminent question. As Lewis said in "Learning in Wartime," "Human life has always been lived on the edge of a precipice. Human culture has always had to exist under the shadow of something infinitely more important than itself." Humans must recognize that they are on a pilgrimage toward "a permanent city satisfying the soul" and should not expect to build a Heaven on earth. So "a man may have to die for his country, but no man must, in any exclusive sense, live for his country. He who surrenders himself without reservation to the temporal claims of a nation, or a party, or a class is rendering to Caesar that which, of all things, belongs emphatically to God: himself."[9]

When Lewis does include a chapter titled "Social Morality" in *Christian Behaviour*, he says explicitly that Christianity has no particular current political agenda. "It could not. It is meant for all men at all times and a particular programme which suited one place or time would not suit another." He then goes on to outline some characteristics of what an ideal Christian society might look like and is careful to point out that it would seem leftist in economic policy but reactionary in expectations for family life and personal behavior, so that it would not come close to any current party agenda. Moreover, he points out that there is little point in talking about a Christian society until "most of us really want it," and that is not going to happen "until we become fully Christian."[10] One cannot embrace the first principle of Christian social morality, "love your neighbor as yourself," until one first learns to love and obey God. So social and political questions drive us back to the prior question of our personal relationship with God.[11]

## 2. He uses common human nature as the point of contact with his audiences

Lewis's lifelong search for timeless truths led him not only to core Christian doctrines but also to an ability to reach wide audiences. How was he able to achieve his common touch? One might think that, as a prototypical university don who spent most of his days buried in books, he would be poorly prepared to communicate with ordinary people. But for Lewis almost the opposite seems to have been the case. His study of literature was integral to his search for common human nature, which was revealed in many guises in differing times and places. So, as he suggested in his sermon "Learning in Wartime," Lewis was like a traveler who had lived in many places. One of the practical implications of that was that his learning shaped his sense of what he had in common with ordinary people who shared in perennial human experience. As Malcolm Muggeridge commented, "As a pilgrim, Lewis is Bunyan's man, rather than Thomas Aquinas's." Muggeridge's point is that Lewis was concerned with Everyman more than with the intellectual's high theorizing. He was a great admirer of Samuel Johnson and shared Johnson's zeal to find the common sense of the race.[12]

Because it is rare to hear of scholars, especially since the era of academic specialization, whose deep academic studies enhance their abilities to communicate with ordinary people, Lewis's resistance to modern trends is worthy of comment. The study of literature as an academic discipline was relatively new in Lewis's day, but even then he could see that the trends toward professionalization were leading toward the dominance of critical theory over appreciation of the literature itself. Lewis was deeply suspicious of theory. So he disdained "the type of critic for whom all the great names in English literature . . . are as so many lampposts for a dog."[13] Quasi-scientific literary theories, like the giant in *The Pilgrim's Regress*, aspired to "see through" things in a sense of explaining them away. Lewis, in contrast, aspired rather to "see through" the eyes of others. His own works of literary criticism focus on alerting readers to what they might *enjoy*. As the reviewer in the *Times Literary Supplement* put it regarding Lewis's monumental *English Literature in the Seventeenth Century, Excluding Drama* (1952), "Mr. Lewis . . . knows how to make his learning *felt*."[14] Readers of *Mere Christianity* have often remarked on this same quality.

Lewis's goal in studying literature was to learn from and to enjoy sharing the experiences of people from many times and places. In reflecting on his approach in *An Experiment in Criticism*, published in 1961, he wrote in his concluding paragraph: "My own eyes are not enough for me, I will see through those of others. Reality, even seen through the eyes of man, is not enough, I will see what others have invented. . . . In reading great literature I become a thousand men and yet remain myself. . . . Here, as in worship, in love, in moral action, and in knowing, I transcend myself; and am never more myself than when I do."[15]

*Mere Christianity* ends on a similar note. Lewis says that as long as you are bothering about finding how Christ might improve your own personality, you will never find him. "The very first step," he writes, "is to try to forget about the self altogether. Your real new self (which is Christ's and also yours, and yours just because it is His) will not come as long as you are looking for it. It will come when you are looking for Him." That might sound strange, but Lewis points out that it is a common principle in all sorts of everyday matters: "Even in social life, you will never make a good impression on other people until you stop thinking about what sort of impression you are making." That same "principle runs through all life from top to bottom. Give up yourself, and you will find your real self." And so he concludes in his final sentences: "Look for yourself, and you will find in the long run only hatred, loneliness, despair, rage, ruin, and decay. But look to Christ and you will find Him, and with Him everything else thrown in."[16]

At the same time that Lewis was alert to common human traits, he was also alert to how these traits related to ordinary people he encountered every day. That aspect of his common touch suggests that he cultivated a similar approach to those whom he saw around him—whether the hired help at home, the staff at the university, shopkeepers, barkeepers, parishioners at the church, soldiers he met on the train or on RAF visits—as he did to persons from the past, to try to see through their eyes. Lewis had an extraordinary imagination, as is evidenced in his ability to create a reality seen through children's eyes in *Narnia*. He seems to have nurtured similar sensibilities toward people unlike himself. That he would do so must have grown out of a conviction that he stated so eloquently in his 1940 sermon "The Weight of Glory": "There are no ordinary people." The same attitude is apparent in his willingness to answer thousands of letters, despite finding that a hugely disruptive chore.

A counterpart to taking seriously all sorts of people in trying to understand human nature was that Lewis looked within himself to understand the human condition and its deepest problems. That sensibility contributed to the intangible qualities of authenticity and personal integrity that come through in *Mere Christianity*. Biographical treatments of Lewis show that almost all the issues he raises are those that he had wrestled with on his own journey. *The Screwtape Letters* reveal his personal knowledge of the obstacles to the faith. A revealing example of how seriously he took his own admonitions is that in the fall of 1940 he began the daunting practice of making formal confessions to an Anglican priest. According to Owen Barfield's estimate, Lewis took moral self-reflection so seriously that "self-knowledge for him had come to mean recognition of his own weaknesses and shortcomings and nothing more."[17]

Another bit of evidence both of integrity and of taking ordinary people seriously was that, as mentioned earlier, Lewis donated to charities most of the income he received from his books and lectures. Lewis's letters to the BBC often contain instructions on where to send his fees. Eventually such informal arrangements became a problem, and Lewis engaged Barfield, who had studied law and become a solicitor in London, to manage his affairs. Barfield testifies that he "gave two-thirds of his income away altogether and would have bound himself to give the whole of it away if I had let him."[18] Such qualities would, of course, be only indirectly perceived by his early audiences but have contributed to his lasting reputation. Yet from the beginning what many people perceived was an authentic voice of one who knew what he was talking about yet was often self-effacing rather than posing as an expert.

Taking ordinary people seriously as not so ordinary is related to Lewis's recognition, which he often emphasized, that to be an effective apologist he had to be a

CHAPTER EIGHT

"translator." Translation was one way of reducing the distances among people and finding a common ground. In order to speak to average unbelieving English people such as one might expect to find in the pubs, one had, like the missionary to Africa, to learn a new language. More broadly, the speaker had to take into account that traditional Christian language had no clear meaning to most of one's audience. That was a problem for churches as well. So Lewis recommended that every examination in theology "ought to include a passage from some standard theological work for translation into the vernacular."[19] As he recommended to a correspondent, "It only involves first writing down in ordinary theological college English exactly what you want to say and then translating," much as though you were turning it into Greek prose.[20] Or, as he put it on another occasion: "Any fool can write *learned* language. The vernacular is the real test."[21]

When Lewis took the assignment to speak on the radio to virtually every sort of person in England, he recognized that, going beyond just finding common linguistic ground, he would have to find his point of contact with his audience in common human experience. One advantage of being a student of literary history who had observed human nature in many times and places was that Lewis had a particularly acute understanding of the peculiarities of how twentieth-century British people thought. Particularly important, he recognized that in the modern world one of the great obstacles to the Christian message was that the culture encouraged people to think they were already good as they were. So Lewis attempted to counter that modern conceit by first appealing to almost universal human convictions regarding fair play and justice and the instinctive belief that there really is a right and a wrong. Once they recognized that such beliefs implied an objective moral law, he might be able to lead them to recognize that that made the existence of a lawgiver probable. Hence, if they themselves sometimes violated that law, the violation might be an actual wrong with serious consequences. So Lewis recognized that he could not start with an explicitly Christian challenge but rather must begin with cultivating a sense of guilt that would be a necessary first step toward seeking a cure.

Lewis's belief that modern people could be brought to recognize an objective right and wrong was grounded in part in his wide study of other cultures through the ages. During the same era that Lewis was doing his broadcasts he was working on a series of lectures, delivered early in 1943 and then published as *The Abolition of Man*. In these Lewis criticized modern British schools for teaching, in effect, that all aesthetic and moral judgments were essentially subjective. He argued, to the contrary, that there were objective moral standards, and one bit of evidence was that similar basic moral precepts could be found in every culture. Despite cultural differences in applications of these standards, there was remarkable agreement in first principles. Lewis provided an appendix in which he illustrated that these moral premises, which he called the Tao (or the Way), could be found in Greek, Roman, Chinese, Babylonian, ancient Egyptian, and Old Norse writings. Throughout history humans have recognized basic moral principles of general and special beneficence, duties to parents, children, ancestors, elders, and posterity, the law of justice, the law of good faith and veracity, the law of mercy, and the law of magnanimity. Lewis only alluded to these commonalities in his broadcasts, but in the final version of *Mere Christianity* he added several sentences summarizing the argument and referring readers to the appendix of *The Abolition of Man*.[22]

In his opening series of broadcasts Lewis made a point of saying that he was not yet presenting any explicitly Christian teaching but rather was appealing to what everyone might understand on their own. "We are not taking anything from the Bible or the Churches," he said, "we are trying to see what we can find out about this Somebody [behind the moral law] on our own steam."[23] He was looking together with his listeners at what they could find out "on our own steam." In twentieth-century England, Lewis recognized that although many people had been exposed to some Christian teaching, often it was only enough to inoculate them against taking it seriously. So he needed to find common ground in the sorts of moral judgments everyone already engaged in.

Much of Lewis's work, especially his fiction, was built around this theme of helping people to recognize that there were moral realities that their own self-centeredness as well as many modern outlooks encouraged them to deny. In *The Screwtape Letters* he exposed the subtle ways in which people rationalize their failures and guilt. The three interplanetary science-fiction novels illustrated how modern scientific ideals and illusions could blind people from recognizing elementary moral realities. And in each of the Narnia tales at least one of the characters is confronted with his or her own guilt. In *The Voyage of the "Dawn Treader,"* for instance, Eustace, who is a know-it-all little prig, perhaps modeled on Lewis himself as a schoolboy, is acting so beastly that he gets turned into a literal dragon. But then "he realized that he was a monster cut off from the whole human race. An appalling loneliness came over him. He began to see the others had not really been fiends at all. He began to wonder if he himself had been such a nice person as he always supposed."[24]

From his own experience and his studies of human nature, Lewis knew that fostering some sort of self-recognition such as Eustace's was a necessary first step in preparation for direct evangelization.

## 3. Lewis sees reason in the context of experience, affections, and imagination

In order to foster such self-recognition among his audience, Lewis realized that he had to appeal to experience, affections, and imagination and not just to reason. As Michael Ward noted in response to John Beversluis, Lewis made a distinction between imagination as "the organ of meaning" and reason as "the natural organ of truth."[25] So, in his view, reason cannot operate independent of the imagination that shapes meaning. Lewis does, of course, use his formidable rational powers but also acknowledges that fully rational people might assess the evidence of Christianity differently.[26] So he recognizes that the best reasoning has to be set in contexts that excite the affections or the deepest loves, desires, fears, and hopes that make up the whole experience of a person.

Commentators on Lewis and *Mere Christianity* have long noticed this feature of his work and described it in a variety of ways. One of the earliest was Austin Farrer, a leading Anglican theologian of the day and a friend of Lewis at Oxford, who commented that "we think we are listening to an argument; in fact, we are presented with a vision; and it is the vision that carries conviction." *Mere Christianity*, Farrer maintained, was not so much a work of apologetics as a display of the moral force of Christianity.[27]

The Yale theologian Paul L. Holmer provided a classic sustained analysis of a similar point, observing that few have combined such a "plea for objectivity with a portrayal with the riches of human subjectivity." Rather than battering his audience with a host of hypotheses and arguments so that they are rendered helpless to decide, Lewis approaches them as active moral agents who are engaged in relationships: "It is as if the argument does not begin to gather its force until the reader has realized something about himself."[28]

J. I. Packer, one of the most revered of British evangelical theologians, ties these qualities, as have many others, to Lewis's combination of imagination and rationality. "The best teachers," writes Packer, "are always those in whom imagination and logical control combine, so that you receive wisdom from their flights of fancy as well as a human heartbeat from their logical analyses and arguments." Packer goes on to remark, "Because Lewis's mind was so highly developed in both directions, it can truly be said of him that all of his arguments (including his literary criticism) are illustrations, in the sense that they throw light directly on realities of life and action, while all his illustrations (including the fiction and fantasies) are arguments, in the sense that they throw light directly on realities of truth and fact."[29]

The essential biographical background for understanding Lewis's combination of appeals both to reason and to the imagination is that his early atheism had been grounded in an overestimation of the powers of reason alone. He later described his most influential and beloved teacher, W. T. Kirkpatrick, or "The Great Knock," as almost "a purely logical entity." Kirkpatrick was also a materialist and an atheist who would not allow for opinions that could not be demonstrated, and he was totally dedicated to the pursuit of rational truth within those bounds. Lewis discovered that once he had adopted such thoroughgoing rationalism he was left with a sharply divided self: "Nearly all that I loved I believed to be imaginary; nearly all I believed to be real I thought grim and meaningless." He came to see that reason such as Kirkpatrick's, which was grounded on the prior assumption of materialism, was a "shallow rationalism."[30] But without abandoning his commitment to rigorous rationality, he sought to reconcile that with the rest of his experience, including his imagination, moral sensibilities, and deepest desires. Traditional Christianity, he eventually discovered, satisfied all these aspects of his experience better than any of the alternatives.

Alister McGrath, himself a popular apologist and also a biographer of Lewis, offers a close analysis of the role reason plays in Lewis's apologetic method. As McGrath and others have observed, Lewis uses reason not to try to *prove* the truth of Christianity but rather to clear away objections and to help him show others that, as he himself discovered, its account of things best fits the whole of their experience. So, for instance, in his chapter "Hope" in *Christian Behaviour*, he argues that the deepest desires and longings that we all have but are never wholly fulfilled in this life are indications that this life is not all there is: "If I find in myself a desire which no experience in this world can satisfy, the most probable explanation is that I was made for another world."[31] Such experiences of desire or longing had been immensely important to Lewis himself in his search for something beyond materialism. Yet the argument is not presented as a proof. Rather, it is "the most probable explanation." Lewis first sketched two other sorts of explanation and then presented the Christian view ("'Creatures are not born with desires unless satisfaction of those desires exists'") as best fitting the whole of our experience. McGrath observes that Lewis's approach is similar to what is today in the philosophy of science called "inference to the best explanation" or looking for the "big picture" that makes the best sense of all our observations.[32] Lewis himself captures the concept in one of his compelling images: "I believe in Christianity as I believe that the sun has risen, not only because I see it, but because by it I see everything else."[33]

In *Miracles*, a more formal apologetic work, Lewis used the analogy that we might possess parts of a novel or a symphony. If someone claimed that a newly discovered manuscript would provide the link on which the whole plot turned or reveal the main theme of the symphony, "Our business would be to see whether the passage, if admitted to the central place which the discoverer claims for it, did actually illuminate all the parts we had already seen and 'pull them together.'"[34] As this analogy suggests, reason would play a prominent and essential role in the process. Yet ultimately what would decide the issue would be a host of considerations that would be intuitive and experiential.

Lewis was deeply aware that modern people were living in a disenchanted universe and that part of what he needed to do was to broaden their sensibilities. In the modern world, shaped in such large measure by

CHAPTER EIGHT

the standards of modern science and technology, many "sensible" people limit their vision to material things that can be measured and managed through instrumental reason. Whereas at one time people had instinctively recognized that everyday reality was packed with personality and meaning, modern culture had taught them to be blind and deaf to all the wonders of reality that surrounded them, including spiritual realities. One of Lewis's memorable depictions of this trait is in the character of Uncle Andrew in *The Magician's Nephew*, the story of the origins of Narnia. Even though Uncle Andrew fancies himself as a magician, he in fact makes thoroughly modern scientific assumptions and is both self-centered and "dreadfully practical." He has no interest in the magical world beyond how he can use it for his own profit. So when Aslan begins to sing a beautiful song, he convinces himself that he is hearing a roar, because "Who ever heard of a lion singing." Unlike the other characters, Uncle Andrew cannot hear Aslan or the other animals speak because he knows that it is impossible for them to do so.[35]

In a famous passage from his sermon "The Weight of Glory," Lewis elicits our deepest sense of beauty, longing, and desire and then asks:

> Do you think I am trying to weave a spell? Perhaps I am; but remember your fairy tales. Spells are used for breaking enchantments as well as for inducing them. And you and I have need of the strongest spell that

can be found to wake us from the evil enchantment of worldliness that has been laid upon us for nearly a hundred years. Almost our whole education has been directed to silencing this shy, persistent, inner voice; almost all our modern philosophies have been devised to convince us that the good of man is to be found on this earth.[36]

In weaving his various spells to break the blinding enchantment of modern disenchantment, Lewis does not in the least denigrate the role of reason. Rather, he uses all his rational powers to expand his audience's abilities to recognize other dimensions of reality beyond those known by instrumental reason alone.

Lewis, then, did not hold a naïve view that people could be led to the faith simply through rational arguments. He trusted in reason and believed that people through the ages shared some common sensibilities and reasoning abilities. Yet he also saw that human reasoning takes place in the context of prior dispositions and assumptions that may block us from recognizing the truth. Lewis was confident that under the right circumstances people could be brought to see that Christianity is fully rational in the sense of providing the best explanation of things, that it is the clue to the puzzle that makes everything else fall into place. Nonetheless, the case for Christianity is not like a mathematical or philosophical proof that all rational people can be compelled to recognize. Rather than a simple set of arguments or just "evidence that demands a verdict,"

*Mere Christianity* rests on an appeal to the experience of the whole person.

Interpreters have recognized this relationship of reason to imagination in describing Lewis's rhetorical strategies. Lewis realized that neither rational appeals by themselves nor emotional appeals by themselves were likely to persuade.[37] James Como, in helpful observations on Lewis's apologetic rhetoric, shows how he typically frames arguments by defining terms, laying out (often dichotomous) alternatives, identifying with the reasonableness of the objections of his audience, and presenting the rational superiority of the Christian alternative while at the same time making that alternative imaginatively and emotionally appealing. In *Mere Christianity* he typically allows some of the steps in what might be a more formal argument to be implied but brings his readers to recognize this same combination of both a best explanation and something that resonates emotionally with their own experiences and desires. Como illustrates the power of this strategy with the testimony of the actress Debra Winger, who co-starred in the movie *Shadowlands*. Winger, although not a Christian herself, had studied Lewis very carefully. In response to a question as to whether, as the film suggests, Lewis was someone who gave "easy" answers to "difficult" questions, Winger replied, "He may make difficult *questions* accessible. I don't think he makes the answers 'easy.'" She added, "He's in that school of discourse where his statements are not like books that are written by experts." Rather, she offered, "He's saying 'think about this.'" As Como summarizes his point, "Lewis's rhetoric is inseparable from his *voice*, both reasonable and rhapsodic, doubly inviting."[38]

## 4. He is a poet at heart, using metaphor and the art of meaning in a universe that is alive

Lewis's views on the interrelationship of reason and the imagination are closely connected to his effective use of images, metaphors, and analogies. This feature is related to his artistry in fiction. It also reflects his sensibilities as someone whose first ambition was to be a poet. In his work as a popular apologist he employs a succession of simple comparisons and metaphors both to clarify the meanings of his rational arguments and to excite the affections or experiential sensibilities of his readers. These devices also allow him to communicate to wide audiences not only in England of the 1940s but across both time and cultures.

Just about everyone who has reflected on the lasting strengths of *Mere Christianity* has noticed its excellence in the use of analogy and metaphor. Michael Ward relates that to Lewis's larger rhetorical strategy of enhancing his rational arguments with analogies that both clarify understanding and add vivid emotional force. Specifically, Ward argues that Lewis avoids the more simply emotive "come-to-Jesus" technique of popular evangelism but rather tells his audience, "This is what it is like to come to Jesus." To illustrate, Ward offers a "brief survey" drawn from *Mere Christianity*:

> Becoming a Christian (passing from death to life) is like joining in a campaign of sabotage, like falling at someone's feet or putting yourself in someone's hands, like taking on board fuel or food, like laying down your rebel arms and surrendering, saying sorry, laying yourself open, turning full speed astern; it is like killing part of yourself, like learning to walk or to write, like buying God a present with his own money; it is like a drowning man clutching at a rescuer's hand, like a tin soldier or a statue becoming alive, like waking after a long sleep, like getting close to someone or becoming infected, like dressing up or pretending or playing; it is like emerging from the womb or hatching from an egg; it is like a compass needle swinging to north, or a cottage being made into a palace, or a field being plowed and resown, or a horse turning into a Pegasus, or a greenhouse roof becoming bright in the sunlight; it is like coming around from anesthetic, like coming in out of the wind, like going home.[39]

Mickey Maudlin, the executive editor for religion at HarperOne, who has overseen the publication of Lewis's works, after offering a similar list of analogies drawn from both Lewis's fiction and his apologetics, emphasizes that in both Lewis is asking you to take an imaginative journey in which you are asked to choose sides. So in *Mere Christianity* readers are not just learning about Christianity or about how to become a better person. Rather, they are being led to see that the narratives of their own lives are set in the midst of a much larger real-life cosmic drama that tells of a loving but dangerous God who is inviting them to be remade.[40]

Chad Walsh, Lewis's first major American promoter, in reflecting on the key role of the analogies "in the seductive power of *Mere Christianity*," suggested that we might "say that they are little poems interspersed in the prose text bringing to full life the ideas that otherwise would smack of the scholar's study." Walsh continues: "Their poetic quality does not make them literally 'true' but it makes them clear and appealing, and helps the reader imagine things that might just possibly be true, no matter how contrary they are to his daily common sense."[41]

Lewis's use of metaphors to engage the imagination was not just a clever skill or strategy but rather reflected his fundamental views of communication and reality itself. "All our truth, or all but a few fragments," he maintains, "is won by metaphor." So, as Michael Ward explains, "We don't grasp the meaning of a word or concept until we have a clear image to connect it with."[42] Moreover, these metaphors point toward realities that are "a kind of psycho-physical parallelism (or more) in the universe."[43] Scientific language, Lewis acknowledges, provides a very useful way of speaking about some things. But most of our meaningful experience is not susceptible to such precise technical analysis. "The very essence of our life as conscious be-ings," he explains, "all day and every day, consists of something which cannot be communicated except by hint, similes, metaphors, and the use of those emotions (themselves not very important) which are pointers to it." These imaginative understandings are not simply about our emotions but about apprehending things in their relationships beyond us. "We are not really con-cerned with the emotions: the emotions *are* our con-cern about something else." So a mother who is wor-ried about her son in the army would not be truly cured by a drug that relieved her anxiety; her over-whelming concern is not her anxiety but rather the safety of her son. "Similarly it is no use offering me a drug which will give me over again the feelings I had on first hearing the overture to *The Magic Flute*. The feelings by themselves—the flutter in the diaphragm—are of very mediocre interest to me. What gave them their value was the thing they were about. So in our Christian experience."[44]

In a vein similar to his concern over the modern dis-enchantment of reality, Lewis worried that modern people were losing their imaginative sensibilities. "Evolution may not have ceased," he speculated, "and in evolution a species may lose old powers as well as acquire—possibly in order to acquire—new ones." Modern people, he observed, were being taught to be-lieve that imagination is "only the presence of mental images" and that emotions are about themselves "as distinct from the things they are about."[45] Near the beginning of *The Abolition of Man* he offered a striking example of what he has in mind when he cites modern schoolbook writers who assert that a poetic statement that a waterfall is "sublime" reflects merely the feelings of the speaker rather than the actual quality of the waterfall.[46]

In Lewis's view, the universe is not dead, as evolved moderns would have it, and is not experienced only through the meanings we arbitrarily impose on it. Rather, it is animate and personal. Ultimately it is related to its Creator and through the Creator to us. Everything is related to everything else. As his close friend Owen Barfield remarked, "Somehow what he thought about everything was secretly present in what he said about anything."[47] So the meanings of all higher things and most of all divine things are best apprehended by metaphor and analogy that point to actual and ultimately personal interrelationships.

Lewis, whose first aspirations and first publications were as a poet, was so thoroughly imbued with this way of seeing and communicating things that to speak by metaphor and analogy was second nature. As a lifelong student of English literature and of words, he was constantly reflecting on ways of "producing new metaphors and revivifying old."[48] So immersed was he in the art of metaphor that it was simply part of the way he thought about things. At the same time he employed his habit of razor-sharp critical reasoning to keep his imagination in bounds. Further, because he was a Christian, those bounds were also shaped by a tradition to which he was deeply committed. Almost like a Mozart of words, Lewis was so thoroughly steeped in a rich tradition, was so much a master of a rational discipline, and so much a lifelong connoisseur of the imagination that he could toss off a series of occasional pieces for broadcast that were not even at first planned to make up a book, and they would turn out to be a compelling set of rhetorical gems.

## 5. Lewis's book is about "mere Christianity"

The most conspicuous trait that helps account for the continuing vitality of the book is that it is about "mere Christianity." As Lewis explained in his preface, he meant to present only "the belief that has been common to nearly all Christians at all times." This "agreed, or common, or central, or 'mere' Christianity" was not to be a watered-down or "vague and bloodless" Christianity but "something positive and pungent." It was ecumenical in the sense of looking for commonalities among Christians of all denominations through the ages. Yet it encouraged readers to affirm the particularities of a specific subtradition but to be generous to those who chose differently.

Though Lewis made clear that he was using "mere" in the older sense of related to an essential or unembellished central core, as a philologist or student of the history of language he must have been aware that many would at first read his title in the far more common modern sense of "merely Christianity." Lewis himself sometimes used "mere" in this more usual diminishing sense, as in a talk in which he responded to modern sophisticates who claimed theology was "*merely* poetry."[49] In a book title, the double meaning worked. If one took it to mean "merely Christianity," the title was suggesting with a touch of irony that there is more to the well-worn doctrines than meets the eye. That was indeed one of Lewis's goals. There was no real conflict with his more positive definition of the title as referring to the essence of the most widely shared Christian teachings. Either way, many would find themselves encountering something far more momentous than they had anticipated.

Aside from the title itself, the conspicuous non-sectarianism and practical ecumenism in the book itself has to be one of the major sources of its continuing appeal. It would be an overstatement to say that the twenty-first century is a "postdenominational age," but perhaps it is heading in that direction. At least it is certain that since Lewis's time denominational loyalties have eroded in many parts of world Christianity. That is especially true for many evangelicals in the United States. Much of American evangelicalism has been shaped by nondenominational parachurch agencies for evangelism, missions, and other forms of outreach. Further, in the past generation, in America and elsewhere, megachurches have often eclipsed older denominations in defining evangelical identity. And people who retain some specific denominational loyalties are more often ready to recognize their commonalties with fellow Christians across institutional lines than they once were. That is also true for many traditionalist Christians who are affiliated with older churches such as the Roman Catholic, Eastern Orthodox, or worldwide Anglican, Presbyterian, Lutheran, Methodist, and Baptist Churches and the like. Among all of these, the idea of "mere Christianity" has a wide appeal and provides the basis for a practical ecumenism that encourages recognition that, despite institutional differences, Christians of many sorts share a core of perennial commitments.

Lewis's resolve to limit his presentation to the essentials of the shared Christianity of the ages was not just a strategy but rather reflected some of his deepest convictions. It was the prize of his quest to rely on timeless truths rather than recent fads. Even in one of his earliest statements about his return to faith, in 1930, he observed that there "are many ways back to the truth," but "no way, faithfully followed, can lead anywhere, at last, except to the centre."[50] Lewis soon identified that center in a set of core teachings found in many traditions and in many eras. Being an Anglican, part of a tradition known for its mediating spirit, he was in a particularly good place to cultivate such perennial sensibilities. It also helped that some of his best friends, especially J.R.R. Tolkien, who helped lead him to Christianity, were Catholic, even if Lewis himself was not attracted to Rome. He cultivated his faith through friendships in an academic setting where what various Christians had in common was far more important than their differences. So a practical ecumenical spirit based on shared traditionalist teachings was close to the heart of his Christian convictions.

Nourished as Lewis was personally on the life-changing sensibilities of perennial Christianity, he found his singular calling. "Since my conversion," he wrote in 1950, "it has seemed my particular task to tell the outside world what all Christians believe."[51] Lewis acknowledged that there was a place for precise theological distinctions and arguments about them, but these were out of bounds when explaining Christianity to outsiders or the wavering. So he believed that it should be a firm rule, as he said in the preface to *Mere Christianity*, that "our divisions should never be discussed except in the presence of those who have already come to believe that there is one God and that Jesus Christ is His only Son." As Patrick T. Ferry has observed, Lewis recognized the danger of churches' seeming to form an exclusive "inner ring." So Lewis's winsomeness as an evangelist is directly related to his having confined his task to inviting everyone to the vestibule and leaving to others all debates about choosing particular rooms.[52] Paradoxically, one result is that Christians of many very different sorts regard Lewis as though he were one of their own. So, as Mickey Maudlin observes, "No matter what kind of Christian group I am in—whether Catholic, mainline Protestant, evangelical, or even Mormon—they describe Lewis as if he were an 'insider' in their circles."[53]

CHAPTER EIGHT

Furthermore, as Maudlin also points out, Lewis's commitment to avoid doctrinal disputes results in an engaging humility in presenting some of the more difficult Christian teachings. Often he will explain a point and then say something like "that is as far as I can go." Or he will avoid a debate by a telling analogy, as, when dealing with the much-disputed relationship of faith to works in salvation, he remarks, "I have no right to speak on such a difficult question, but it does seem to me like asking which blade in a pair of scissors is most necessary."[54]

## 6. *Mere Christianity* does not offer cheap grace

It is crucial to recognize that "mere Christianity" is not minimal Christianity. It is not comfortable or "safe." It is not, to use the term that Dietrich Bonhoeffer coined in the same era, "cheap grace." Rather, readers find that they are being drawn in to an understanding of Christianity that is going to be extraordinarily demanding of them personally. They are being asked to give up their very "self" as a sovereign entity and to experience Christ living in them: "To become new men means losing what we now call 'ourselves,'" Lewis writes. "Out of our selves, into Christ, we must go." He continues: "This is the whole of Christianity. There is nothing else. . . . The Church exists for nothing else but to draw men into Christ, to make them little Christs." We are being made into creatures who can obey the command, "Be ye perfect." We are to be transformed "from being creatures of God to being Sons of God." That is possible only if we are "in Christ," who is the first instance of this new humanity. So there must be "a real giving up of the self."[55]

David Meconi, SJ, has offered the clarifying insight that Lewis's emphasis on becoming "little Christs" is the key to understanding the unifying purpose of *Mere Christianity*. Employing his many metaphors, such as catching a "good infection" or turning a horse into a winged creature or simply taking seriously the implication of saying that God is "Our Father," Lewis is vivifying an ancient Christian theme of being remade by being drawn into the life of the Trinity. Pride is "the great sin" because it is the opposite: the belief of self-made persons that they need no dependence on others. And, as Lewis explains, Christian behavior is "more like painting a portrait than like obeying a set of rules." You must be "seriously trying to be like Christ," with "the real Son of God . . . at your side," and receiving life from him so that you are "beginning to turn the tin soldier [of yourself] into a live man."[56]

Lewis's simple but demanding emphasis on giving up one's old self to have Christ live within is, characteristically, a refreshing way to get to the heart of the matter. The teaching of being "in Christ" has enough evident basis in the Bible and in every church tradition for people readily to recognize that it is authentic—one of those things about which they say: "Of course that's what it's all about." They are likely to see it as both immensely appealing and immensely challenging. Without spelling out the details, it suggests that having Christ dwell within must be a matter of God's grace but that giving up the sovereignty of the old self will not come without a struggle. Only some readers, of course, will be attracted to that message and its demands. But almost all serious readers will recognize that they have encountered something weighty.

7. The lasting appeal of *Mere Christianity* is based on the luminosity of the Gospel message itself

In 1939 Lewis published an essay titled "The Personal Heresy in [Literary] Criticism." He argued that it was wrong to view a poem as about the poet's state of mind. "The poet is not a man," he wrote, "who asks me to look at *him*; he is a man who says 'look at that' and points; the more I follow the pointing of his finger the less I can possibly see of *him*."[57]

Lewis would have said the same for his work as an apologist. Had it drawn primary attention to himself or been just a reflection of his own peculiar views, it would have had little lasting impact. His own role need not be minimized in saying that. His character, integrity, and sometimes self-effacing authority shine through. And, in the United States especially, the fact that he was a scholar who taught at Oxford and Cambridge carries a lot of weight and is often offered as one explanation of his American popularity. Yet, as Dallas

Willard has observed, "He never pulls authority on you." Rather, he speaks with the authority of someone who himself has discovered something and wants to show it to others.[58] So, granting that there is an aura of prestige around Lewis himself, one of the greatest sources of the lasting vitality of his presentations is that he very deliberately points the listener or reader toward an object beyond himself. As others have observed, he does not simply present arguments; rather, he acts more like a friendly companion on a journey. To expand on that image: he is like a companion on a hike who is a learned but companionable naturalist and who points out all sorts of flora or tiny flowers or rock formations that you would have missed on your own. When you see these wonders you are duly impressed with your guide as an intermediary, but, particularly if he leads you around a bend where you encounter the most astonishing mountain peaks set against stunning lakes that you have ever seen, your attention is overwhelmed by the beauty of the objects themselves. You are deeply grateful to your guide, but that is not the essence of your unforgettable encounter with that luminous beauty. So Lewis points his audiences toward seeing Christianity not as a set of abstract teachings but rather as something that can be seen, experienced, and enjoyed as the most beautiful and illuminating of all realities.

CHANGES IN *MERE CHRISTIANITY* COMPARED
TO THE ORIGINAL THREE BOOKS

See Phillips, *Time of War*, appendix 2, 303–7, for a chart comparing the order and title of the broadcasts with the chapters in the publication. Walter Hooper in his introduction to *Mere Christianity: An Anniversary Edition* (New York: Macmillan, 1981), xx–xxxii, and Phillips, *ibid.*, each provide comparisons of surviving broadcast scripts to the publications, and I have summarized their significant findings in chapter 2.

In preparing *Mere Christianity* from the three earlier works, Lewis did some minor editing throughout. He dropped contractions and most italics and changed things like "last week" in the radio addresses to "last chapter." There are some other verbal changes, although most paragraphs are identical to the originals.

Here are the notable changes:

Lewis's new preface replaced those of *Broadcast Talks* and *Beyond Personality* (as I have described in chapter 4).

In book 1, chapter 1 (1:1), he added an early new paragraph saying that there are several types of laws of nature, such as the law of gravity, but the moral law is the only one humans are free to disobey. He also added a sentence referring readers to the appendix of *The Abolition of Man*, which shows how major cultures had shared many common basic moral principles.

In 2:1 he dropped a paragraph regarding its being inconsistent to trust your thinking if you disbelieve in God (as I have summarized and quoted in chapter 4).

In 2:2 he added the present third paragraph regarding people who knock down simple versions of Christianity but then complain about the complexity if you point them to something less simple. He also changed "Reality, in fact, is always something you could not have guessed" to "Reality, in fact, is usually something you could not have guessed."

In 2:3 he added two paragraphs regarding Jesus's claims (as I have noted in chapter 4).

In 2:4, "The Perfect Penitent," he added a paragraph answering the objection that because Jesus was God it was too easy for him to suffer as a human. This paragraph was an expansion of a point he made in a letter of October 15, 1951 (*Letters*, 3:143), to Wendell W. Waters, who had raised this objection. The letter and the revision contain the example that one being rescued from drowning would not complain that the person on the shore casting out the rope had an unfair advantage.

In 3:5, "Sexual Morality," in addition to the changes I have noted in chapter 4, he added a paragraph defending against some criticisms the analogy in which he argued that the popularity of striptease in modern culture illustrated that something has gone wrong with the sexual appetite in the same way that, if there were a culture whose people got their thrills through slowly uncovering a delicious meal on stage, one would conclude something was wrong with their appetite for food.

*Beyond Personality* was not substantially changed from the original publication.

## ACKNOWLEDGMENTS

My first debt is to the staff of the Marion E. Wade Center at Wheaton College in Wheaton, Illinois. They were extraordinarily helpful in aiding me in this work. I am especially grateful to the late director, Christopher P. Mitchell, to whom this book is dedicated. Marjorie Lamp Mead was similarly gracious and insightful during early discussion of the project. I also benefited from the extremely knowledgeable and gracious aid of Laura Schmidt, the Center's archivist. Shawn Mrakovich provided valuable assistance as well. The Wade Center was also helpful in making inquiries, including on their Web site, regarding the use of *Mere Christianity* around the world. I am especially grateful and honored to have been the 2013 recipient of the Clyde S. Kilby Research Grant from the Wade Center. I highly value the esteem of those who work at this fine center, and it has been a pleasure to work with them.

A number of scholars and others have been particularly helpful in making suggestions or furnishing me with materials prior to formal publication. These include Stephanie Derrick, Alan Jacobs, Bruce L. Johnson, Alister McGrath, Robert Millett, Bill Reimer, and Michael Ward. Mickey Maudlin, religion editor at

HarperOne, has been helpful in sharing his own reflections on Lewis as well as other information.

Maggie Noll provided invaluable research materials that greatly enriched this work concerning early Lewis reception. Mark Noll offered insights on that material, as well as on much else about Lewis.

I am grateful to all those who contributed to the project of trying to discover where *Mere Christianity* is used throughout the world. I have thanked these contributors in the long note near the end of chapter 6. I want, however, to express my gratitude again for those who especially facilitated that effort or provided extensive comments. These include Daniel Denk, Philip George, Philip Holtrop, John McIntosh, Majorie Lamp Mead, Steven Van Zanen, and Yongmei Wang.

I am deeply grateful to my editor, Fred Appel, who invited me to contribute to this series and has been unwaveringly helpful in seeing the project to its end. I also thank my copy editor, Marilyn Martin, for her excellent and sympathetic work. Debbie Tegarden and Juliana K. Fidler of Princeton University Press were always most helpful and efficient. I am also grateful for Julie Shawvan's good work on the index.

As always, my greatest debt is to my wife, Lucie. We have each weathered some storms healthwise since this project began and I think value each other's love and support even more as a result.

## ABBREVIATIONS AND SHORT TITLES FOR NOTES

WORKS BY C. S. LEWIS:

*Christian Reflections.*    Refers to *Christian Reflections*, edited by Walter Hooper (Grand Rapids: William B. Eerdmans, 1967).

*God in the Dock.*    Refers to *God in the Dock: Essays on Theology and Ethics*, edited by Walter Hooper (Grand Rapids: William. B. Eerdmans, 1970).

*Letters.*    Refers to *The Collected Letters of C. S. Lewis*, edited by Walter Hooper, vol. 1, *Family Letters, 1905–1931* (HarperSanFrancisco, 2004); vol. 2, *Books, Broadcasts, and the War, 1939–1949* (HarperSanFrancisco, 2004); and vol. 3, *Narnia, Cambridge, and Joy, 1950–1963* (HarperSanFrancisco, 2007).

*MC.*    Refers to *Mere Christianity*. Because it has been published in many versions, references to it in the notes are by book and chapter (e.g., 3:2) only. The

|  | standard current English version is *Mere Christianity: A Revised and Amplified Edition, with a New Introduction, of the Three Books,* Broadcast Talks, Christian Behaviour, *and* Beyond Personality (San Francisco: HarperOne, 2001 [1952]). |
| --- | --- |
| *The Screwtape Letters.* | Because this book is also found in many editions, it will be referred to by the number of the "Letter" only (e.g., "Letter 3"). The standard current English version is *The Screwtape Letters, with Screwtape Proposes a Toast* (San Francisco: HarperOne, 2001). *The Screwtape Letters* was first published as a book in 1942 (London: Geoffrey Bles). |
| *Surprised by Joy.* | Refers to *Surprised by Joy: The Shape of My Early Life* (London: Collins, Fontana Books, 1959). Originally published in 1955 (London: Geoffrey Bles). |

SECONDARY WORKS

These works are also suggested starting points for further readings.

| *Cambridge Companion.* | Refers to *The Cambridge Companion to C. S. Lewis,* edited by Robert MacSwain and Michael |
| --- | --- |

Ward (Cambridge, England: Cambridge University Press, 2010).

Green and Hooper, *Biography*.
Refers to Roger Lancelyn Green and Walter Hooper, *C. S. Lewis: A Biography* (New York: Harper, Brace, Jovanovich, 1974).

Holmer, *C. S. Lewis: The Shape of His Faith and Thought*.
Refers to Paul L. Holmer, *C. S. Lewis: The Shape of His Faith and Thought* (New York: Harper and Row, 1976).

Hooper, *Guide*.
Refers to Walter Hooper, *C. S. Lewis: A Complete Guide to His Life and Works* (HarperSanFrancisco 1996). Originally published under the title *C. S. Lewis: A Companion and Guide*.

Jacobs, *Narnian*.
Refers to Alan Jacobs, *The Narnian: The Life and Imagination of C. S. Lewis* (San Francisco: HarperOne, 2005).

*Lightbearer*.
Refers to *C. S. Lewis: Lightbearer in the Shadowlands; The Evangelistic Vision of C. S. Lewis*, edited by Angus J. L. Menuge (Wheaton, IL: Crossway, 1997).

McGrath, *A Life*.
Refers to Alister E. McGrath, *C. S. Lewis: A Life; Eccentric Genius, Reluctant Prophet* (Carol Stream, IL: Tyndale, 2013).

McGrath, *Intellectual World*.
Refers to Alister E. McGrath, *The Intellectual World of C. S. Lewis*

|                           | (West Sussex, England: Wiley-Blackwell, 2014). |
| Phillips, *Time of War*.   | Refers to Justin Phillips, *C. S. Lewis in a Time of War: The World War II Broadcasts That Riveted a Nation and Became the Classic* Mere Christianity (San Francisco: HarperOne, 2002). |
| *Pilgrim's Guide*.         | Refers to *The Pilgrim's Guide: C. S. Lewis and the Art of Witness*, edited by David Mills (Grand Rapids: William B. Eerdmans, 1998). |

In the notes, C. S. Lewis is referred to as CSL when citing *Letters*. The parts of *Mere Christianity* are cited using book and chapter numbers; for instance, 1:2 refers to book 1, chapter 2. All italics are in the original quotations.

INTRODUCTION

1. "Books of the Century: Leaders and Thinkers Weigh in on Classics That Have Shaped Contemporary Religious Thought," *Christianity Today*, April 24, 2000, 92–93.
2. David Biema, "Religion Beyond the Wardrobe," *Time*, October 30, 2005, http://content.time.com/time /magazine/article/0,9171,1124316,00.html.
3. Lewis, *Surprised by Joy*, 55.
4. C. S. Lewis, *The Problem of Pain*, in *The Complete C. S. Lewis Signature Classics* (San Francisco: HarperOne, 2002), 568.
5. Jacobs, *Narnian*, 75.
6. Quoted in Jacobs, *Narnian*, 78.
7. Lewis, *Surprised by Joy*, 167.
8. *Ibid.*, 178.
9. *Ibid.*, 171.
10. *Ibid.*, 178–79.
11. *Ibid.*, 181–82.

12. McGrath, *A Life*, 138.

13. McGrath (in *ibid.*, 141–46) makes a convincing case that Lewis misdated this step as being taken in the spring of 1929.

14. CSL to Greeves, October 18, 1931, *Letters*, 1:977. Of the many accounts, I have followed most closely McGrath's recent and insightful one, in *A Life*, 131–59, except in his attempt to redate to the spring of 1932 Lewis's experience, while riding to Whipsnade Zoo, of finding himself believing in Christ's divinity. The letters to Greeves of October 1 and 18, 1931, far outweigh the consideration that Lewis referred to spring flowers when he mentioned "the bluebells underfoot," which may well have been simply a poetic expression.

15. Cf. Hooper's summary, *Guide*, 184.

16. Lewis, *The Problem of Pain* (1940), quotations from 551 and 552.

CHAPTER ONE
War Service

1. CSL to Greeves, September 15, 1939, *Letters*, 2:274.

2. Winston S. Churchill, *The Second World War*, vol. 2, *Their Finest Hour* (Boston: Houghton Mifflin, 1976 [1949]), 32.

3. Churchill, speech to the House of Commons, June 4, 1940, available at WinstonChurchill.org, http://www .winstonchurchill.org/resources/speeches/1940-the -finest-hour/we-shall-fight-on-the-beaches.

4. CSL to Dom Bede Griffiths, OSB, July 16, 1940, *Letters*, 2:423.

5. Robert E. Havard, "*Philia*: Jack at Ease," *C. S. Lewis at the Breakfast Table, and other Reminiscences*, edited by James T. Como (New York: Macmillan, 1979), 220.

6. Havard, "*Philia*," 222.

7. CSL to Brother George Every, SSM, October 12, 1940, *Letters*, 2:448.

8. James Welch to CSL, February 7, 1941, quoted in Phillips, *Time of War*, 80.

9. From a translation of the Latin dedication (1931) to Phillips, *Time of War*, 16.

10. Kenneth M. Wolfe, *The Churches and British Broadcasting: The Politics of Broadcast Religion, 1922–1956* (London: SCM, 1984), 66–75.

11. Phillips, *Time of War*, 39. Angus Calder, in *The People's War: Britain 1939–1945* (London: Granada, 1971), 551, reports a survey in a section of London at the end of the war in which three quarters of the women and two-thirds of the men said they believed in God, but six in ten never went to church.

12. Wolfe, *Churches and British Broadcasting*, 170–91.

13. Adrian Hastings, *A History of English Christianity, 1920–2000* (London: Collins, 1986), 40 (referring to around the 1920s). Robert Currie et al., in *Church and Churchgoers: Patterns of Church Growth in the British Isles since 1700* (Oxford: Clarendon, 1977), report that in 1940 there were about 2.5 million Catholics in England and Wales and a total of about 3 million in Great Britain. In Great Britain in 1940 (when the population was just under 50 million), the "church membership" numbers are reported as 2.255 million Anglicans, 1.311 million Scottish Presbyterians, and 1.874 million Nonconformists. "Annual Church Membership in Britain, 1900–1970," 25.

14. Phillips, *Time of War*, 83–84.

15. Walter Hooper, in the introduction to *Mere Christianity: An Anniversary Edition* (New York: Macmillan,

1981), xi, says he probably never owned a radio and tried to stay out of earshot of them.

16. Welch to CSL, February 7, 1941, in Phillips, *Time of War*, 80.

17. CSL to Welch, February 10, 1941, *Letters*, 2:470.

18. Keith Robbins, "Britain, 1940 and Christian Civilization," in *History, Religion and Identity in Modern Britain* (London: Hambledon, 1993), 195–213.

19. George Orwell and I. Angus, eds., *The Collected Essays, Journalism and Letters of George Orwell* (London, 1968), 17–18, quoted in Robbins, "Britain, 1940," 213.

20. Hooper, *Guide*, 268.

21. Hooper, *Guide,* 304n.

22. Harry Lee Pole, "C. S. Lewis was a Secret Government Agent," *Christianity Today,* December 10, 2015. http://www.christianitytoday.com/ct/2015/december-web-only/cs-lewis-secret-agent.html CSL to Greeves, May 25, 1941, *Letters*, 2:486.

23. Babbage, "To the Royal Air Force," in *C. S. Lewis: Speaker and Teacher*, edited by Carolyn Keefe (Grand Rapids: Zondervan, 1971), 65 and 69.

24. CSL to Sister Penelope, CSM, May 15, 1941, *Letters*, 2:485 and 485n.

25. CSL to Dorothy Sayers, April 1942, *Letters*, 2:515.

26. CSL to Greeves, December 23, 1941, *Letters*, 2:504.

27. Babbage, "To the Royal Air Force," 68.

28. Lewis, "God in the Dock," in *God in the Dock*, 242–43.

29. CSL to Sister Penelope, May 15, 1941, *Letters*, 2:484–85.

30. McGrath, *A Life*, 209.

CHAPTER TWO
Broadcast Talks

1. Phillips, *Time of War*, 117–18. For a popular account of Lewis and the broadcasts, see Paul McCusker, *C. S. Lewis and Mere Christianity: The Crisis that Created*

a *Classic* (Carol Stream, IL: Tyndale House, 2014). A dramatized version of the story is also available on CD: *C. S. Lewis at War: The Dramatic Story Behind Mere Christianity* (Colorado Springs, CO: Focus on the Family Radio Theatre, 2013).

2. George Sayer, *Jack: C. S. Lewis and His Time* (San Francisco: Harper and Row, 1988), 168. Phillips, in *Time of War*, 119, reports a similar recollection, from John Lawler, of Lewis's reception in an RAF mess where everyone stopped to listen.

3. Walter Hooper, introduction to *Mere Christianity: An Anniversary Edition of the Three Book* (New York: MacMillan, 1981), xv. Both Hooper and Phillips have compared the original transcripts to the publications and pointed out any notable differences.

4. *MC* 1:5.

5. Phillips, *Time of War*, 119.

6. *MC* 1:2.

7. Fenn to CSL, September 4, 1941, quoted in Phillips, *Time of War*, 135. CSL to Fenn, September 7, 1941, *Letters*, 2:491.

8. Hooper, note, *Letters*, 2:483.

9. CSL to Arthur Greeves, December 23, 1941, *Letters*, 2:504.

10. Jacobs, *Narnian*, 224

11. CSL to Fenn, February 25, 1942, *Letters*, 2:509–10.

12. CSL to the Reverend Joseph Dowell, November 30, 1941, *Letters*, 2:498.

13. Hooper, note, *Letters*, 2:498.

14. Reproduced from the original transcript in Hooper, introduction to *Mere Christianity: An Anniversary Edition*, xvii–xviii. The original preface to *Broadcast Talks: Reprinted with Some Alterations from Two Series*

of *Broadcast Talks* ("Right and Wrong: A Clue to
the Meaning of the Universe" and "What Christians
Believe"), *Given in 1941 and 1942* (*The Case for Christianity* in the United States) (London: Geoffrey Bles,
1942), condenses this original and leaves out being
blown "sky-high" and the medical analogy.

15. Fenn to CSL, December 3, 1941, *Letters*, 2:499.

16. Cf. his sermon "The Weight of Glory": "Do you think
I am trying to weave a spell? Perhaps I am . . . ," in *The
Weight of Glory, and Other Addresses*, edited by Walter
Hooper (New York: HarperCollins, 1980), 31. (Cf. my
chapter 8.)

17. *MC* 2:3. See the discussions of this argument in chapters 6 and 7 of this book.

18. *MC* 2:5.

19. Fenn to CSL, February 18, 1942, in Phillips, *Time of
War*, 153.

20. CSL to Fenn, August 15, 1942, *Letters*, 2:528.

21. See, for instance, Angus Calder, *The People's War:
Britain 1939–1945* (London: Granada, 1982 [1969]),
esp. 305–8.

22. CSL to Sister Penelope, November 9, 1941, *Letters*,
2:496.

23. CSL to Dorothy Sayers, April 1942 [no day], *Letters*,
2:515. Cf. to Sister Penelope, October 24, 1940, *Letters*,
2:451.

24. Quoted from Phillips's interview with Jill Freud,
November 19, 1999, in Phillips, *Time of War*, 180.

25. CSL to Sister Penelope, October 24, 1940. He
told Hooper of the cold feet. Green and Hooper,
*Biography*, 198.

26. Phillips, *Time of War*, 160.

27. *MC* 3:1.

28. *MC* 3:5.

29. CSL to Fenn, November 30, 1942, in Phillips, *Time of War*, 167.

30. See Phillips, *Time of War*, 305, on a comparison of the broadcasts and chapters. The chapter "Christian Marriage" in *Mere Christianity* also expands the section on "being in love" from one paragraph in the original book, *Christian Behaviour*, to six.

31. *MC* 3:2.

32. Green and Hooper, *Biography*, 210, quoting a review in the *Tablet* (June 26, 1943), n.p.

33. Bruce R. Johnson, "C. S. Lewis and the BBC's *Brains Trust*: A Study in Resiliency," *SEVEN: An Anglo-American Literary Review*, November 2013, 79–80. Lewis's largest audiences were for his second (1.7 million) and third (2.1 million) broadcasts, delivered on August 13 and 20, 1941. Johnson observes that when Lewis appeared as a guest on the *Brains Trust* show in 1942, it drew over 5 million listeners for each of two shows. "Don v. Devil," *Time*, September 8, 1947, 67, reports that each talk was heard by about 600,000 people, a figure that is widely repeated but is far too modest. Only Lewis's very first broadcast had an audience that small.

34. Stephanie L. Derrick, in "The Reception of C. S. Lewis in Britain and America," Ph.D. dissertation, University of Sterling, 48, cites the following with the same subtitle: Wright, *The Average Man: Broadcast Talks* (London: Longman, Green, 1942); Fred Townley Lord, *A Man's Religion: Series of Four Broadcast Talks on the B.B.C. Forces Programme* (London, 1940); Walter

Carey, *As Man to Man: Broadcast Talks to the Forces* (London: A. R. Mowbray, 1940); W. A. L. Elmslie, *Five Great Subjects: Broadcast Talks, etc.* (London: SCM, 1943), preface; and J. H. Oldham, ed., *The Church Looks Ahead: Broadcast Talks* (London: Faber and Faber, 1941), 340–374. On Wright, see also Wolfe, *Churches and British Broadcasting*, 278–80. Wolfe reports (269) that Wright's audiences eventually numbered around 7 million, a figure that, as Derrick observes, makes Lewis's audience seem modest by comparison. I am indebted to Derrick for sharing with me a draft of her revised book manuscript, "Chronicling Fame: the Reception of C. S. Lewis in Britain and America."

35. Hooper, *Guide*, 309.
36. CSL to Greeves, [January 1943], *Letters*, 2:549.
37. See Phillips, *Time of War*, 221–31, for an account of exchanges between Lewis and the BBC leading to these broadcasts.
38. McGrath, *A Life*, 197–99.
39. CSL to Fenn, April 12, 1943, *Letters*, 2:568.
40. Phillips, *Time of War*, 225–27. The BBC records do not include Lewis as having appeared on this program of July 22, recorded on July 19. Lewis, however, did have a script of the discussion and may have pulled out at the last minute. See Phillips, *Time of War*, appendix 3, 308–11, for the text of this script.
41. Fenn to CSL, May 6, 1943, in Phillips, *Time of War*, 227–28.
42. CSL to Fenn, May 7, 1943, *Letters*, 2:571–72.
43. CSL to Fenn, June 16, 1943, *Letters*, 2:581.
44. CSL to Fenn, July 1, 1943, *Letters*, 2:583.
45. Phillips, *Time of War*, 243–44.

46. CSL to Fenn, February 10, 1944, *Letters*, 2:602.

47. *MC* 4:1.

48. *MC* 4:8. Phillips, *Time of War*, 253–54.

49. "C. S. Lewis's Surviving BBC Address," YouTube.com, http://www.youtube.com/watch?v=JHxs3gdtV8A.

50. See Phillips, *Time of War*, appendix 4, 306–7, for a chart comparing the seven broadcasts, the seven *Listener* publications (with slightly different titles), and the eleven chapters of the book versions.

51. CSL to Fenn, March 25, 1944, *Letters*, 2:608–9. Lewis responded to one letter in *The Listener* that had accused him of preparing the way for a return to the burning of witches. He pointed out that he was against religious compulsion of any kind and had protested against "the intolerable tyranny of compulsory church parades for the Home Guard." CSL, "To the Editor of *The Listener*, [published March 9, 1944], *Letters*, 2:605–6. But he pulled a broader "apologia," observing that "replies, except in a real rigorous high-brow controversy, are always a mistake." CSL to Fenn, April 4, 1944, 2:610. A version of this apologia is likely found in "Two Notes," which is chapter 6 of the published editions of *Beyond Personality*.

52. Fenn to Lewis, March 31, 1944, in Phillips, *Time of War*, 255.

53. Fenn to Lewis, March 23, 1944, in Phillips, *Time of War*, 254.

CHAPTER THREE
Loved or Hated

1. CSL to Fenn, April 4, 1944, *Letters*, 2:610.

2. CSL to Fenn, March 25, 1944.

3. Fenn to Lewis, November 10, 1942, quoted in Phillips, *Time of War*, 172.

4. *Freethinker*, November 1, 1942, 449–50.

5. George Orwell, "As I Please," *Tribune*, October 27, 1944, http://www.telelib.com/authors/O/OrwellGeorge/essay/tribune/AsIPlease19441027.html. I am indebted to Stephanie Derrick for pointing me to this review.

6. *Times Literary Supplement*, September 19, 1942, 460.

7. "Theology as Discovery: Mr. C. S. Lewis's Talks," review of *Beyond Personality: The Christian Idea of God*, *TLS*, October 21, 1944, 513. See Hooper, *Guide*, 327–28, for summaries of some other reviews. Bruce L. Edwards, in *C. S. Lewis: Life, Works, and Legacy* (Westport, CT: Praeger, 2007), 3:67–68, quotes some additional reviews.

8. G. D. Smith, "Nature and Spirit, According to a Recent Work," *Clergy Review*, February 1945, 69. Specifically, Smith held that Lewis's account at the beginning of chapter 5 of *Beyond Personality*, which said that the fallen state of humans involved the natural self-centered life distorting our spiritual sensibilities, needed to be replaced with a Catholic doctrine regarding the supernatural endowments of humans lost at the Fall and restored in salvation."

9. R. L. De Wilton [of Macmillan Publishers USA] to Edward A. Golden, New York City, December 3, 1943, Wade Center Archives, Wade Center, Wheaton College, Wheaton, IL.

10. R. C. Churchill, "Mr. C. S. Lewis as an Evangelist," *Modern Churchman*, January–March, 1946, 334. Churchill quotes a number of such reviews in church periodicals, without exact references.

11. Lee, *C. S. Lewis and Some Modern Theologians* (London: Lindsey, 1944), 4, 10, and 11–16.

12. E. L. [Edgar Leonard] Allen, "The Theology of C. S. Lewis," *Modern Churchman*, January–March 1945, 317–24, quotations from 318–321.

13. Churchill, "Mr. C. S. Lewis as an Evangelist," 334–42, quotations from 335, 341, and 342.

14. Sayers to Mrs. Robert Darby, May 31, 1948, *Letters of Dorothy L. Sayers*, vol. 3, edited by Barbara Reynolds (Cambridge, England: The Dorothy L. Sayers Society, 1998), 135, quoted in Samuel Joeckel, *The C. S. Lewis Phenomenon: Christianity in the Public Sphere* (Macon, GA: Mercer University Press, 2012), 269.

15. On his earliest reception, cf. Mark Noll's paper "C. S. Lewis in America: 1933–1947," presented at a conference at Wheaton College, Wheaton, IL, in October 2013. My account of Lewis's American reception up to the mid-1950s is dependent on the thorough research of Maggie Noll. I am most grateful to these valued friends for sharing their work with me.

16. "Books—Authors," *New York Times*, July 8, 1943, 17.

17. P. W. Wilson, *New York Times Book Review*, March 28, 1943, 3.

18. "Sermons in Reverse," *Time*, April 19, 1943, 76.

19. Leonard Bacon, "Critique of Pure Diabolism," review of *Screwtape*, *Saturday Review*, April 17, 1943, 20.

20. De Wilton to Golden, June 16, 1943, December 3, 1943, and March 3, 1944, Wade Center Archives. In November 1948, Chad Walsh wrote, "Twentieth Century Fox is considering the possibilities of extracting a movie from Screwtape." Preface to *C. S. Lewis: Apostle to the Skeptics* (New York: Macmillan, 1949), ix.

21. "Reluctant Believer," *Time*, January 24, 1944, 96. The sales figures suggest that *Screwtape* had already sold even better in America than in Great Britain. De Wilton reported that *Screwtape* had sold seventy thousand copies in Great Britain since February 1942. CSL to Golden, June 16, 1943, Wade Center Archives.

22. Leonard Bacon, "The Imaginative Power of C. S. Lewis," review of *Perelandra*, *Saturday Review*, April 8, 1944, 9.

23. Forman, "Common-Sense Humanist," *NYTBR*, April 23, 1944, 12.

24. Wilson, "Prophecy Via BBC," *NYTBR*, July 22, 1945, 8.

25. Cooke, "Mr. Anthony at Oxford," *New Republic*, April 24, 1944, 578–80.

26. Ibid.

27. Ibid.

28. Based on Maggie Noll's wide-ranging search of American periodicals, the only strongly negative comment in the general press seems to have been that of John Haynes Holmes, a Universalist pastor and editor and a reviewer for the *New York Herald Tribune Book Review*, who, while praising the first half of *The Case for Christianity* (November 14, 1943, 42), describes the second book as involving "an almost incredibly naïve statement of Christian theology." Oddly, however, Holmes's brief review of *Beyond Personality* in the same journal (September 23, 1945, 12), has only praise for Lewis for the "magic" of "his clarity of thought and simplicity of expression."

29. Charles Keenan, review of *The Case for Christianity*, *America*, September 18, 1943, 664, and James J. Maguire, CSP, review of the same, *Catholic World*, November 1943, 215–16.

30. Anne Freemantle, review of *Beyond Personality*, *Commonweal*, September 14, 1945, 528 and 529; Harold C. Gardiner, SJ, review of *Beyond Personality*, *America*, May 26, 1945, 158–59; and Philip J. Donnelley, SJ, "Protest on C. S. Lewis," *America*, June 30, 1945, 263.

31. Malachi J. Donnelly, SJ, "Church Law and Non-Catholic Books," *American Ecclesiastical Review*, June 1946, 403–9, quotations from 406 and 408.

32. As in the anonymous comment under "Books Received" regarding *Beyond Personality*, *Christian Century*, June 20, 1945, 734. Cf. an anonymous brief review in *Christian Century*, September 29, 1943, 1105; Talmage C. Johnson, review of *The Problem of Pain*, *Christian Century*, December 1, 1943, 1400; and an anonymous brief review of *Christian Behaviour*, *Christian Century*, January 26, 1944, 114.

33. Poling, editor's comment, *Christian Herald*, December 1943, 70.

34. Walter F. Whitman, review of *Christian Behaviour*, *Anglican Theological Journal*, July 1944, 191.

35. Myers, "The Religious Works of C. S. Lewis," review, *Theology Today*, January 1, 1945, 545–48, quotations from 545 and 548.

36. Anderson, "C. S. Lewis: Foe of Humanism," *Christian Century*, December 25, 1946, 1562–63. Cf. a wholly positive review of *Miracles: A Preliminary Study*, by Gaius Glenn Atkins, *Christian Century*, December 3, 1947, 1486–87.

37. Unsigned review, *Moody Monthly*, December 1943, 239.

38. *Moody Monthly*, May 1944, 536. Cf. the largely positive but cautious unsigned review of *Beyond Personality* in the *Sunday School Times*, October 5, 1946, 914–15.

39. C. S. Lewis, "How I Know God Is," *His*, February 1944, 11–13. Cf. the very positive review of *Screwtape* by editor Virginia Lowell, *His*, January 1946, 21–22.

40. Woolley, review of these two books and *The Problem of Pain*, *Westminster Theological Journal*, May 1944, 210–14, quotations from 210 and 213.

41. Eppinga, review of *Beyond Personality*, *Westminster Theological Journal*, May 1946, 225–27, quotation from 226.

42. Van Til, review of *Beyond Personality*, *United Evangelical Action*, May 15, 1946, 21. For Van Til's fuller critique, see his *Defense of the Faith* (Philadelphia: Presbyterian and Reformed Publishing, 1955, 75–77. See also "The Theology of C. S. Lewis," an unpublished manuscript largely about *Mere Christianity*, available at WordPress.com, http://presupp101 .wordpress.com/2012/08/23/the-theology-of-c-s -lewis-by-cornelius-van-til/.

43. *United Evangelical Action*, June 15, 1946, 15.

44. Walsh, "C. S. Lewis, Apostle to the Skeptics," *Atlantic Monthly*, September 1946, 115–19, quotations from 119.

45. Elton Trueblood, *While It Is Day* (New York: Harper and Row, 1971), 68 and 99–101. Cf. James R. Newby, *Elton Trueblood: Believer, Teacher, and Friend* (New York: Harper and Row, 1990), 67–68.

46. For example, "World Seen Split by Two Ideologies," *New York Times*, July 18, 1949, 15, reporting on a sermon by an Episcopal leader, the Reverend Leland B. Henry, and mentioning Lewis among those helping to turn the West back from godlessness.

47. "Don v. Devil," *Time*, September 8, 1947, 65–74, http://content.time.com/time/magazine/article

/0,9171,804196,00.html. Lewis's observations on fashions is from his 1946 address "The Decline of Religion," in *God in the Dock*, 218–23.

48. Paul Jordan-Smith, "I'll Be the Judge, You Be the Jury," *Los Angeles Times*, October 9, 1949, D5.

49. Nash K. Burger, "Of Modern Books and Living Faiths," *NYTBR*, December 25, 1949, 1.

50. On neo-Thomism, or neo-Scholasticism, as a passing fashion, see, for instance, CSL to Dom Bede Griffiths, January 6, 1936, *Letters*, 2:176.

51. Walsh, *C. S. Lewis: Apostle to the Skeptics*, quotations from 12, 13, and 73. See also 73–75 and 166–68.

CHAPTER FOUR
A Classic as an Afterthought

1. "Don v. Devil," 74.

2. CSL to John Beddow, October 7, 1945, *Letters*, 2:673–74. See Phillips, *Time of War*, 260–79, for Lewis's declination of almost all broadcasts—except a dramatization of *The Great Divorce*.

3. "Christian Apologetcs," in *God in the Dock*, 103. Lewis says much the same thing in a letter to Dorothy Sayers (August 2, 1946, *Letters*, 2:730).

4. Hooper, *Guide*, 343–44.

5. Harry Blamires, "Teaching the Universal Truth: C. S. Lewis among the Intellectuals," *Pilgrim's Guide*, 16.

6. For some detail on the early project, see George Sayer, *Jack: C. S. Lewis and His Time* (San Francisco: Harper and Row, 1988), 308–9 and 312–13.

7. Cf. Christopher W. Mitchell, "C. S. Lewis and the Oxford Socratic Club," in *Lightbearer*, 329–52, esp. 342–43, and Walter Hooper, "Oxford's Bonny

Fighter," in *C. S. Lewis at the Breakfast Table, and Other Reminiscences*, edited by James T. Como (New York: Macmillan, 1979), 137–85. Humphrey Carpenter, in *The Inklings: C. S. Lewis, J. R. R. Tolkien, Charles Williams and Their Friends* (Boston: Houghton Mifflin, 1979), 217, suggested that Lewis may have changed course due to the Anscomb debate, and A. N. Wilson, in *C. S. Lewis: A Biography* (New York: Harper Collins, 1990), 210–14, provides a strong version of it. The *Journal of Inkling Studies*, October 2011, 9–123, provides a symposium on the philosophical issues of the Anscombe–Lewis exchange.

8. Jacobs, *Narnian*, 235.

9. Ward, *Planet Narnia: The Seven Heavens in the Imagination of C. S. Lewis* (New York: Oxford University Press, 2008), 214–22. Ward, however, more than Jacobs, sees the turn to Narnia as, at least in part, a response to the Anscombe debate.

10. Lewis, *Broadcast Talks*, 37–38.

11. See chapters 7 and 8.

12. *Letters*, 3:213n.

13. CSL to John H. McCullum, October 1, 1956, *Letters*, 3:791. The original subtitle in the United States included *The Case for Christianity* rather than *Broadcast Talks*. In twenty-first-century editions, "Enlarged" has been changed to "Amplified" in the subtitle.

14. *The Screwtape Letters*, Letter 25.

15. Lewis, "On the Reading of Old Books," in *God in the Dock*, 201–2.

16. Richard Baxter, *Church History of the Government of Bishops and Their Councils, Abbreviated* (1681), xiv.

17. *Broadcast Talks*, 5.

18. *Beyond Personality*, 5–6.

19. CSL to Peter Milward, SJ, July 4, 1955, *Letters*, 3:628.

20. See chapter 7 for reactions to this argument.

CHAPTER FIVE
Into the Evangelical Orbit

1. Although Geoffrey Bles continued to publish the volume and had offered a second printing by 1955, those British sales were soon eclipsed by those of the Collins publishing house, which offered a mass-market paperback Fontana Books edition in 1955, which was in its tenth impression by 1963. Macmillan issued a Colliers mass-market edition in 1960 and also a trade paperback in 1962 that became the best-selling edition over the next few decades. By 1965 Macmillan was offering a sixteenth printing (apparently of its original edition) and by 1967 was into the eight printing of another edition (presumably the paperback). The heavy American sales appear to have begun in the 1970s. *Publishers Weekly*, August 13, 1982, 47, reports that Macmillan had sold 1.620 million copies since issuing it as a trade paperback in 1962. Cf. chapter 6, note 1. See also WorldCat, Abe Books, and Goodreads for listings of editions and printings, including those from a number of other publishers over the years. *The Case for Christianity* was published as a separate volume as late as 1996 by Touchstone Books, Simon and Schuster. The latest printing of *Christian Behavior* as a separate volume is from Geoggrey Bles in 1963, and the latest of *Beyond Personality* is from Bles in 1959 (according to WorldCat listings).

2. Kathleen Nott, *The Emperor's Clothes* (London: William Heiemann, 1953), quotations from 8, 48, and 312.

In addition to such dismissals of the popular apologetics, Nott included a lengthy critique of Lewis's argument in *Miracles* that naturalism is self-refuting because of the unreliability of reason that it entails (258–84).

3. Tom Driberg, "Lobbies of the Soul," *New Statesman and Nation*, March 19, 1955, 393–94.

4. Walsh, "Impact on America," in *Light on C. S. Lewis*, edited by Jocelyn Gibb (London: Geoffrey Bles, 1965), 111–13.

5. Lewis, "Cross-examination," interview with Shirwood Wirt, May 7, 1963, in *God in the Dock*, 265, originally published in *Decision*, September 1963, 3, and October 1963, 4.

6. See Elesha J. Coffman, *The Christian Century and the Rise of the Protestant Mainline* (New York: Oxford University Press, 2013), 189–200.

7. Kenneth Dole, "Seminarian Assails Billy Graham Work," *Washington Post and Times Herald*, June 14, 1955, 30.

8. W. Norman Pittenger, "Apologist versus Apologist: A Critique of C. S. Lewis as 'Defender of the Faith,'" *Christian Century*, October 1, 1958, 1104–1107.

9. Ibid.

10. Ibid.

11. C. S. Lewis, "Rejoinder to Dr. Pittenger," *Christian Century*, November 26, 1958, 1359–61. This is also found in *God in the Dock*, 177–83. Pittenger offered a reply, published as a letter in the *Christian Century*, in which he agreed that there had long been a need for "translators" of the faith for the common person. Nonetheless, he insisted that always keeping an eye

out for "what Jones will take" was a "very *bad* modernism." Apologists had to commend the faith, "but at the same time to commend it in absolute integrity of mind—with guarding of style, with nuances, with fine shades, with ambiguity, at those place where these things are indicated as essential to a fully truthful presentation of the faith." "Letters to the Editor," *Christian Century*, December 24, 1958, 1486.

12. Ibid.

13. Clyde S. Kilby, *The Christian World of C. S. Lewis* (Grand Rapids: William B. Eerdmans, 1964), 5. Even strict fundamentalists might enlist Lewis as at least a co-belligerent. Bob Jones II, president of the ultrafundamentalist Bob Jones University in South Carolina, visited Lewis in Oxford shortly after World War II and pronounced him, despite his smoking and drinking, "a Christian." Green and Hooper, *Biography*, 229.

14. CSL to Carl F. H. Henry, September 28, 1955, *Letters*, 3:651. This exchange occurred prior to the meeting with Graham (November 5, 1955), which may have helped soften Lewis's attitude.

15. CSL to Kilby, November 2, 1958, *Letters*, 3:985.

16. CSL to Carl Henry, December 1, 1958, *Letters*, 3:992–93.

17. "John Stott," InterVarsity Press Web page, https:// www.ivpress.com/cgi-ivpress/author.pl/author_id=82.

18. Stott, *Basic Christianity* (Grand Rapids: William B. Eerdmans, 1958), 139.

19. "C. S. Lewis Dead; Author, Critic, 64," *New York Times*, November 26, 1963, 18. This obituary provides the figure of a million copies. William White, in *The*

*Image of Man in C. S. Lewis* (Nashville: Abingdon, 1969), 26, says, without an exact reference, "A London obituary announced that Lewis' paperback sales alone were in the vicinity of one million in England, and provides the sales estimates of 270,000 for *Mere Christianity* and 250,000 for *Screwtape*. *The Problem of Pain* also sold almost 120,000."

20. Walsh, "Impact on America," 115.

21. Bob Smietana, "C. S. Lewis Superstar," with additional reporting by Rebecca Barnes, quoting Hooper from an interview, *Christianity Today*, December 9, 2005, http://www.christianitytoday.com/ct/2005/december /9.28.html?paging=off.

22. Peter Kreeft, *C. S. Lewis: A Critical Essay* (Front Royal, VA: Christendom College Press), 5.

23. "This Week," *Christian Century*, December 30, 1970, 1566. The reviewer did allow room for a Lewis revival, saying, "Since 'transcendence' is making a strong comeback, perhaps Lewis too will have a new inning."

24. Holmer, *C. S. Lewis: The Shape of His Faith and Thought* (New York: Harper & Row, 1976). Two significant volumes of this era, both from mainline Protestant publishers, are Richard B. Cunningham, *C. S. Lewis: Defender of the Faith* (Philadelphia: Westminster, 1967), and William Luther White, *The Image of Man in C. S. Lewis* (Nashville: Abingdon, 1969). Although these both provide some summary and commentary regarding *Mere Christianity*, neither provides significant insight in the way that Holmer's volume does.

25. Holmer, *C. S. Lewis*, ix, 1, and 3.

26. Ibid., 5; cf. 6–7.

27. Ibid., 8, 86, 108, and 115.

28. Kilby, *The Christian World of C. S. Lewis*, 159; cf. 147–72.

29. Keith Hunt and Gladys Hunt, *For Christ and the University: The Story of InterVarsity Christian Fellowship of the USA, 1940 to 1990* (Downers Grove, IL: InterVarsity Press, 1992), 111.

30. "C. S. Lewis and InterVarsity," InterVarsity.org, December 7, 2005, http://www.intervarsity.org/news/c-s-lewis-and-intervarsity.

   Bill Bright, founder of Campus Crusade for Christ, cited Lewis's "trilemma" argument (discussed in my chapter 7) in a widely used pamphlet, "Jesus and the Intellectual," first published in 1959, available at http://www.cru.org/how-to-know-god/jesus-and-the-intellectual/02-man-myth-god.htm. But although that argument was very widely employed by Campus Crusade, that agency does not seem in its early years to have promoted Lewis's own works as much as InterVarsity did. I am grateful to John G. Turner, biographer of Bright, for confirming this impression by e-mail on August 21, 2014.

31. Walsh, foreword to William Luther White, *The Image of Man in C. S. Lewis* (Nashville: Abingdon, 1969), 7.

32. Lewis, *C. S. Lewis: Five Best Books in One Volume* (Washington, DC: Canon, 1969). One intriguing feature of this volume, which went through a number of printings from various publishers in the next few years, was that the five books were *The Screwtape Letters*, *The Great Divorce*, *Miracles*, *The Case for Christianity*, and *Christian Behaviour*. For some reason *Beyond Personality*, book 4 of *Mere Christianity*, was

omitted, indicating that at that late date *Mere Christianity* had not yet fully established its iconic identity as a single volume. Whether the breaking up of *Mere Christianity* represented doctrinal concerns, issues of publishing permissions, or something else is not clear.

33. Lindsell, foreword to *Five Best Books*, vi–vii. On Lindsell, Lewis, and inerrancy, cf. James L. Wall, "C. S. Lewis and Evangelical Ambivalence," *Wittenberg Door*, August–September 1981, 20–25.

34. Donald T. Williams, review of *Real Presence: The Holy Spirit in the Works of C. S. Lewis*, by Leanne Payne (Westchester, IL: Cornerstone, 1979), and Michael J. Christensen, *C. S. Lewis on Scripture* (Waco, TX: Word Books, 1979), *Christianity Today*, May 2, 1980, 38. Williams disparaged "Lewis's own naïvete concerning what is at stake in the doctrine of inerrancy."

CHAPTER SIX
Many-Sided *Mere Christianity*

1. Daisy Maryles, compiler, "Trade Paperback High Rollers," *Publishers Weekly*, August 13, 1982, 46–47. The average of 80,000 per year over twenty years suggests some increase since the early 1970s. In 1974 it was reported ("Chuck Colson's Leveler," *Newsweek*, November 9, 1974, 73) that Americans had bought 100,000 copies in the past eighteen months, so the rate was about 66,700 per year (but presumably that included all editions). A good guess is that the sales were considerably under the 80,000 average for this edition in the 1960s and correspondingly higher than the average in the early 1980s. Apparently the sales steadily increased to the numbers they would

eventually reach (something like 250,000 per year for all the HarperOne English versions in first decade of the twenty-first century). Cf. *Publishers Weekly*, October 10, 1994, 31, where *Mere Christianity* is listed fourth among "Religion Bestsellers" and *Screwtape* is eighth.

2. "The Man Who Converted to Softball," *Time*, June 17, 1974, 16.

3. Charles W. Colson, *Born Again* (Old Tappan, NJ: Chosen Books, 1976), 108–30, quotations from 113. The passages from *Mere Christianity* that Colson quotes are from 3:8.

4. Colson, *Born Again*, quotations from 125, 127, 129, and 130.

5. *Newsweek*, October 25, 1976.

6. Jonathan Aitken, *Charles W. Colson: A Life Redeemed* (New York: Doubleday, 2005), 290–91.

7. "C. S. Lewis Testimonials," file, Wade Center. Cf. the summary of these testimonies in Philip Ryken, "Winsome Evangelist: The Influence of C. S. Lewis," in *Lightbearer*, 68–72.

8. Olford, quoted in Ryken, "Winsome Evangelist," 56, from a video interview of Olford, November 7, 1983, Wade Center. After just a few years of talking to people about Lewis, I find Olford's estimate, based on far more contacts, entirely plausible.

9. Francis S. Collins, *The Language of God: A Scientist Presents Evidence for Belief* (New York: Free Press, 2006), 21.

10. N. T. Wright, "Why Left, Right & Lewis Get It Wrong," ReadtheSpirit.com,http://www.readthespirit .com/explore/nt-wright-interview-why-left-right

-lewis-get-it-wrong/#sthash.P6doYagh.dpuf. See also some of Wright's criticisms in my chapter 7.

11. Wright, *Simply Christian: Why Christianity Makes Sense* (San Francisco: HarperCollins, 2006). See also N. T. Wright, "Simply Lewis: Reflections on a Master Apologist after 60 Years," *Touchstone*, March 2007, http://touchstonemag.com/archives/article.php?id =20–02–028-f.

12. Anthony Sacramone, "An Interview with Timothy Keller," *First Things*, February 25, 2008, http://www .firstthings.com/onthesquare/2008/02/an-interview -with-timothy-kell; Jonathan Parnell, "When (Seem- ingly) Opposites Meet, Tim Keller and John Piper on C. S Lewis," DesiringGod.org, http://www.desiring god.org/articles/when-seemingly-opposites-meet -keller-and-piper-on-lewis; and John Piper, "Keller and Piper Talk Lewis," DesiringGod.org, http://www .desiringgod.org/blog/posts/keller-and-piper-talk-c-s -lewis. Piper, himself a highly influential pastor and a prolific writer living in Minneapolis, has written an e-book tribute to Lewis, *Alive to Wonder: Celebrat- ing the Influence of C. S. Lewis*, DesiringGod.org, http://www.desiringgod.org/books/alive-to-wonder. Piper came to know and love Lewis's work when at Wheaton College in the 1960s and as a student of Clyde S. Kilby. He writes that he puts Lewis among "the top three writers who have influenced how I read and respond to the world" (1). Like Keller, Piper combines an admiration of Lewis with a great love for the theology of Jonathan Edwards.

13. McGrath, *A Life* and *Intellectual World*.

14. McGrath, *Mere Apologetics* (Grand Rapids: Baker Books, 2012), 12.

15. "Christian Leaders and Books That Have Had Most Influence on Their Lives," Grace Awakening Web site, http://graceawakening.faithsite.com/content.asp ?SID=263&CID=68273. The eight are Brian McLaren, Howard Hendricks, Os Guinness, Chuck Swindoll, C. John Miller, Peter Rossoni, and Chuck Colson. See also Mary Anne Phemister and Andrew Lazo, *Mere Christians: Inspiring Stories of Encounters with C. S. Lewis* (Grand Rapids: Baker Books, 2009), which provides over fifty such stories from prominent Christians, including George Gallup Jr., David Lyle Jeffrey, Michael Ware, and Philip Yancey.

16. D. Michael Lindsay, *Faith in the Halls of Power: How Evangelicals Joined the American Elite* (New York: Oxford University Press, 2007), 90.

17. "The Best Christian Book of All Time: One Year Later," *Emerging Scholars* blog, http://blog.emerging scholars.org/2014/02/the-best-christian-book-of-all -time-one-year-later/#prettyPhoto[13583]/0/.

18. Joseph Pearce, "C. S. Lewis and Catholic Converts," *Catholic World Report*, November 19, 2013, http://www .catholicworldreport.com/Item/2724/cs_lewis_and _catholic_converts.aspx. Cf. Pearce, *C. S. Lewis and the Catholic Church* (San Francisco: Ignatius Press, 2003), for helpful reflections on Lewis's relation to Catholicism.

19. Ibid.

20. Walker Percy, foreword to *The New Catholics: Contemporary Converts Tell Their Stories*, edited by Dan O'Neill (New York: Crossroad, 1987), xv. Also cited by Pearce in "C. S. Lewis and Catholic Converts."

21. Mark Oppenheimer, "Ross Douthat's Fantasy World," *Mother Jones*, January–February 2010, quoted in Pearce, "C. S. Lewis and Catholic Converts."

22. Mariah Blake, "How an Eccentric Right-Wing Billion-aire's Attempt to Build a Catholic Law School Ended in Disaster," *Washington Monthly*, August 20, 2009, http://www.alternet.org/story/142499/how_an_eccentric_right-wing_pizza_billionaire%27s_attempt_to_build_catholic_law_school_ended_in_disaster?page=0%2C0. Cf. Thomas c. Monagham, "C. S. Lewis's Impact on My Faith," in Phemister and Lazo, *Mere Christians*, 175–76 ("dream house" quotation).

23. Pearce, "C. S. Lewis and Catholic Converts."

24. Most explicitly in Thomas Howard, *The Achievement of C. S. Lewis* (Wheaton, IL: Howard Shaw, 1980).

25. Dwight Longenecker, *More Christianity: Finding the Fullness of the Faith*, foreword by Thomas Howard (San Francisco: Ignatius, 2010), 17–39.

26. Francis Beckwith, *Return to Rome: Confessions of an Evangelical Catholic* (Grand Rapids: Brazos, 2009).

27. John Mallon, "A Conversation with Walter Hooper," from *Crisis* magazine, July–August 1994, http://john mallon.net/Site/Walter_Hooper.html.

28. Christopher Derrick, *C. S. Lewis and the Church of Rome: A Study in Proto-ecumenism* (San Francisco: Ignatius, 1981), 181, 200, and 201. David Mills, in "No Mere Christianity," *First Things*, October 18, 2010, http://www.firstthings.com/web-exclusives/2010/10/no-mere-christianity, also says "mere Christianity" is a Protestant concept.

29. Ian Kerr, "'Mere Christianity' and Catholicism," in *C. S. Lewis and the Church: Essays in Honour of Walter Hooper*, edited by Judith Wolfe and B. N. Wolfe (London: T. and T. Clark, 2011), 131.

30. Longenecker, *More Christianity*. Cf. his foreword to
    Pearce, *C. S. Lewis and the Catholic Church*, ix and x.
    W. Patrick Cunningham, in "The Delusion of Mere
    Christianity," *Homiletic and Pastoral Review*, May 1999,
    http://www.catholic.net/rcc/Periodicals/Homiletic
    /May 1999/delusion.htlm, argues from a Catholic per-
    spective that Lewis's imprecision has mostly, although
    not wholly, negative effects.

31. Andrew Walker, "Under the Russian Cross: A
    Research Note on C. S. Lewis and the Eastern Ortho-
    dox Church," in *A Christian for All Christians: Essays
    in Honour of C. S. Lewis*, edited by Andrew Walker
    and James Patrick (London: Regnery, 1990), 63. Ware,
    "C. S. Lewis, and "Anonymous Orthodox?," in Pearce,
    *C. S. Lewis and the Church*, 135.

32. Kallistos Ware, "God of the Fathers: C. S. Lewis and
    Eastern Christianity," *Pilgrim's Guide*, 53–69, quota-
    tion from 69.

33. Mark A. Noll, "C. S. Lewis's 'Mere Christianity' (the
    Book and the Ideal) at the Start of the Twenty-first
    Century," *SEVEN, An Anglo-American Literary
    Review* 19 (2002), 31–44.

34. For a Protestant example, see J. Todd Billings, "The
    Problem with *Mere Christianity*," *Christianity Today*,
    February 2007, 46–47. The article is subtitled "We Jet-
    tison 'Non-essential' Theology at Our Own Peril."

35. Noll, "C.S. Lewis's 'Mere Chrisitianity.'" Michael H.
    Macdonald and Mark P. Shea, in "Saving Sinners and
    Reconciling Churches: An Ecumenical Meditation
    on *Mere Christianity*, in *Pilgrim's Guide*, 43–52, make
    much the same point. They also note (48) the explicit
    use of idea of "mere Christianity" by Charles Colson

as a basis for the cooperative initiative Evangelicals and Catholics Together, begun in 1994.

36. Douglas LeBlanc, "Mere Mormonism," interview with Richard Ostling, *Christianity Today*, February 7, 2000, http://www.christianitytoday.com/ct/2000/february 7/8.72.html.

37. Daniel K. Judd, "C. S. Lewis: Self-Love and Salvation," In *C. S. Lewis: The Man and His Message*, edited by Andrew C. Skinner and Robert L. Millet (Salt Lake City: Bookcraft, 1999), 61–72. Judd, a professor of ancient scripture at Brigham Young University, says that the passage in *Mere Christianity* (4:7) in which Lewis describes sins with the image of "rats in the cellar" had "more influence on me and on my personal conversion to Christianity than anything else C. S. Lewis ever expressed" (69).

38. Millet, "The Theology of C. S. Lewis: A Latter-day Saint Perspective," typescript of a paper presented at the Seventh Annual Wheaton Theology Conference, Wheaton College, Wheaton, IL, April 16, 1998. I am indebted to the author for this typescript and for correspondence regarding *Mere Christianity* in LDS circles. Cf. his "Introduction: C. S. Lewis: The Man and His Message," in *C. S. Lewis: The Man and His Message*, 1–19. Millet writes that he has received little or no criticism from Mormons regarding his views on Lewis but strong critiques from evangelicals. E-mail to the author, January 13, 2014.

39. Mike W. Perry, "Appendix A: C. S. Lewis Resources," in *The C. S. Lewis Readers' Encyclopedia*, edited by Jeffrey D. Schultz and John G. West Jr. (Grand Rapids: Zondervan, 1998), 435–44.

40. Almost all the publications that provide a public record of responses to *Mere Christianity* come from the United States or Great Britain. The book is also popular in evangelical communities in other parts of the former British Empire, such as Australia and Canada.

41. The Reverend Philip George, "C. S. Lewis 'Mere Christianity' Behind the Iron Curtain," e-mail account to the author, August 1, 2014. Marsh Moyle, a Christian evangelist in Eastern Europe for many years, reports that a version was smuggled in significant quantities into Czechoslovakia under Communism.

42. From a compilation of comments including those from Miro Jurik, Milan Cicel, and Pavel Raus gathered by Sarah Liechty in an e-mail to the author, December 5, 2014. I am grateful to the many who have contributed to gathering evidence regarding the use of *Mere Christianity* outside the English-speaking world.

I am especially grateful to the following: to Daniel Denk of InterVarsity Christian Fellowship for his numerous inquiries among the world networks of the International Fellowship of Christian Students, especially in Eastern Europe; to Professor John A. McIntosh of Sydney, Australia, for his inquiries among some forty missionaries from countries including Burma, Cambodia, Ethiopia, Indonesia, France, Germany, Ireland, Italy, Kenya, Rwanda, and Tanzania; to Steven Van Zanen of Christian Reformed World Missions for inquires among their missionaries; to Colin Duriez for identifying translators and publishers in Western Europe; to Colin MacPherson for information regarding publications in Bulgarian, Czech, Macedonian, Serbian, and Tartar; to Dane

Vidovic regarding Serbian publication; to James Sire for some helpful observations; to Martin Haizmann regarding German use of *Mere Christianity*; to Marsh Moyle regarding Bulgarian, Czech, Hungarian, and Russian publication and use; to David Bahena regarding Latin American use; and to Jonathan Lamb (United Kingdom), David Gifford (Mexico), John Vander Stoep (Haiti), Harold Kallemeyn (France), Jeff Bos (Bangledesh), Gerald de Vuyst (Ukraine), Troy Bierma (Nepal), Denis McIntyre (Japan), and a number of other anonymous respondents. I am especially grateful to the Wade Center, particularly to Marjorie Mead and Shawn Mrakovich for posting a request on their Web site asking for information regarding use of *Mere Christianity* abroad. I am also grateful to Mary L. G. Theroux, David Beckmann, Robert Trexler, and Robert MacSwain for posting the inquiry on the Web sites of various C. S. Lewis societies.

Based on publishing information and the results of these unscientific inquiries, I have formed the following additional impressions: *Mere Christianity* has not been much used in non-English-speaking Africa. It has not been translated into any African language except Afrikaans. It has been translated into Portuguese and Spanish, as have many of Lewis's books, but there are no reports of more than moderate usage of *Mere Christianity* in Spain, Portugal, or Latin America (thanks to Juliana K. Fidler for Spanish publication figures). The situation is comparable in Western Europe, where the book has been available in most languages. In South Korea, where there is a large, well-educated Christian population, Lewis is well known, but *Mere Christian-*

*ity* appears to be only moderately used. (Thanks to Byunghoon Woo for furnishing me information to that effect from the largest Korean Christian Internet bookstore in an e-mail sent November 7, 2013.) In Japan, where Christianity is less common, *Mere Christianity* appears to have only scattered use. Other languages in which it has been published include Albanian, Estonian, Indonesian, Lithuanian, Slovene, Thai, and Turkish. I am grateful to Mickey Maudlin of HarperOne and to Laura Schmidt of the Wade Center for lists of non-English publications.

43. "Most likely to have read" is from Phillip Holtrop, a theologian from Calvin College, who also furnishes the final quotation as "typical" (e-mail to the author, May 1, 2013). The publication information and other quotations from online sources are furnished by a translator, Yongmei Wang (e-mail to the author, September 10, 2014). The information about Professor He is from an e-mail from a Chinese editor, Chun'an Li, forwarded by Jin Li to the author September 29, 2014. The same e-mail includes a forwarded e-mail from another editor, Zhiyue Xu, adding some additional details. I am grateful to all those who helped in providing this information.

44. Hitchens, *God Is Not Great* (London: Atlantic Books, 2007), 118, quoted by Stephanie Derrick in "The Reception of C. S. Lewis in Britain and America," 296.

45. This is according to *Wikipedia*, https://en.wikipedia .org/wiki/The_Chronicles_of_Narnia_(film_series).

46. "A Service to Dedicate a Memorial to C. S. Lewis, Writer, Scholar, Apologist," service program, Westminister Abbey (London: Barnard and Westwood,

2013). I am grateful to Michael Ward, a participant in
the service, for sending me a copy of the program.

CHAPTER SEVEN
Critiques

1. Margaret P. Hannay, *C. S. Lewis* (New York: Frederick
   Ungar, 1981), 265–66.
2. John Beversluis, "Preface to the Second Edition,"
   in *C. S. Lewis and the Search for Rational Religion*,
   revised and updated (Amherst, NY: Prometheus,
   2007 [1985]), 10. Peter Kreeft, for instance, refers to
   Beversluis's work as the "abomination of desolation,"
   in *C. S. Lewis: A Critical Essay* (Front Royal, VA:
   Christendom College Press, 1988), 5. Thomas V. Mor-
   ris's review of Beversluis's book in *Faith and Philosophy*, July 1988, 319–22, offers an example of a more
   dispassionate but largely negative critique.
3. Christopher Derrick reports receiving hostile responses
   from some Lewis fans when he commented favorably on Beversluis's book in a review. Derrick, "Some
   Personal Angles on Chesterton and Lewis," in *G. K.
   Chesterton and C. S. Lewis: The Riddle of Joy*, edited by
   Michael H. McDonald and Andrew A. Tadie (Grand
   Rapids: William B. Eerdmans, 1989),10.
4. Beversluis, "Preface to the Second Edition," 23, quoting from *MC* 3:11.
5. Beversluis, *C. S. Lewis and the Search for Rational
   Religion* (Grand Rapids: William B. Eerdmans, 1985),
   2 (2nd ed., 24).
6. Cf. Beversluis, *Search*, 2nd ed., 73–74, and his
   stronger version of this objection in the 1st ed., 37,
   where he says of Lewis, "First, he consistently presents

alternatives to his own views as being perfectly absurd, and second, he consistently presents the absurd view as the only alternative to his own."

7. Beversluis, *Search*, 1st ed., 41.

8. Beversluis also deals at length with other of Lewis's arguments, including his "argument from desire," which appears briefly in *Mere Christianity* in 3:10 but is prominent in other of his works; the argument from reason (that in naturalistic outlooks we have no basis to trust our reason), developed mostly in *Miracles*; and Lewis's arguments regarding the problem of evil, as found largely in *The Problem of Pain*. Beversluis raised the ire of many Lewis partisans not only by his philosophical arguments but also by claiming that Lewis may have lost his faith, or at least his confidence in his faith, after the death of Joy Davidman Lewis.

9. Beversluis, *Search*, 2nd ed., 105–6.

10. Ibid., 111–41. An equally negative but far less sustained critique is found in A. N. Wilson's controversial *C. S. Lewis: A Biography* (London: HarperCollins, 1991 [1990]). Wilson says that it was "when a carapace of intellectual laziness was hardening upon him" that he entered into apologetics (62). The only specific argument Wilson examines critically is the "trilemma" (163–66), but he characterizes Lewis's apologetic works as "breezy" (187), and particularly the broadcast talks as addressing major issues "with a breeziness and a self-confidence which on an academic podium would have been totally unacceptable" (180).

11. Reppert, *C. S. Lewis's Dangerous Idea* (Downers Grove, IL: InterVarsity Press, 2003). See also David Baggett, Gary R. Habermas, and Jerry L. Walls, eds.,

*C. S. Lewis as Philosopher: Truth, Goodness, and
Beauty* (Downers Grove, IL: InterVarsity Press, 2008),
in which Reppert and others update their arguments
partly in the light of Beversluis's second edition.

12. Reppert, *Dangerous Idea*, 36–44; quotation from
Lewis on 38–39 from "Obstinacy of Belief," in *Philoso-
phy of Religion: An Anthology*, 3rd ed., edited by Louis
Pojman (Belmont, CA: Wadsworth, 1998), 390.

13. For another critical assessment of Lewis's arguments,
see Erik J. Wielenberg, in *God and the Reach of Reason: C. S. Lewis, David Hume, and Bertrand Russell*
(Cambridge, England: Cambridge University Press,
2008), who quotes as his epigraph Lewis's remark
about "fully rational minds" disagreeing and provides
carefully reasoned nonpolemical critiques arguing that
Lewis's principal arguments, although not without
merit, are not successful in the sense of providing logi-
cally decisive reasons why Christianity must be true.

14. From Lewis, "Bluspels and Flalansferes: A Semantic
Nightmare" (1939), in *Selected Literary Essays*, edited
by Walter Hooper (Cambridge, England: Cambridge
University Press, 1969), 265, quoted in Michael Ward,
"The Good Serves the Better and Both the Best: C. S.
Lewis on Imagination and Reason in Apologetics,"
in *Imaginative Apologetics: Theology, Philosophy and
the Catholic Tradition*, edited by Andrew Davidson
(London: SCM, 2011), 61–62; cf. 59–78.

15. CSL to Arthur Greeves, October 18, 1931, *Letters*,
1:976–77, quoted in Ward, "Good Serves the Better,"
64–65.

16. Cf. J. T. Sellars, *Reasoning beyond Reason: Imagination as a Theological Source in the Work of C. S. Lewis*

(Eugene, OR: Pickwick, 2011), e.g., 18–22, regarding *Mere Christianity*.

17. The most important sympathetic interpreter to dissent from this view is the literary scholar Ralph Wood, who sharply separates Lewis's imaginative works from his apologetics and says that in his apologetic works, including *Mere Christianity*, "Lewis sometimes regards Christian faith as a set of intellectual propositions" and that his "rationalist proofs" are "among his weakest writings." Wood, "The Baptized Imagination: C. S. Lewis's Fictional Apologetics," *Christian Century*, August 30–September 6, 1995, 812. In Wood's view, Lewis believed that "because these truths [of Christianity] can be rationally demonstrated, they should command assent of all fair-minded people." "C. S. Lewis and the Ordering of Our Loves," *Christianity and Literature*, Autumn 2001, 109–17. Stanley Joeckel, in *The C. S. Lewis Phenomenon: Christianity and the Public Sphere* (Macon, GA: Mercer University Press, 2013), presents a complex version of such a view in which Lewis emerges as simply inconsistent in his views of reason. Joeckel's central thesis is that as a "public intellectual" Lewis adopted "the rules of the liberal-Enlightenment paradigm," which Joeckel sees as involving a basic "evidentialism" assuming universal reason (138). But he also recognizes that Lewis is "indebted to Augustine, who . . . helps give shape to concepts of preconditionalism" (that is, that reasoning is conditioned by prior commitments). Joeckel attempts to explain this tension in terms of a change in Lewis, especially in the 1950s, or as "Hesitant Steps beyond the Public Sphere," as he titles one chapter of

his book. Yet he notes that the preconditionalism is already present in *Mere Christianity* (184–85).

18. Ward, "Good Serves the Better," 71. Cf. McGrath, *Intellectual World*, 135, who says: "Lewis's argument here, as elsewhere, is fundamentally *inductive*, aiming to show how the Christian faith can 'fit in' our experiences of life."

19. Greene and Hooper, *Biography*, 200.

20. Chesterton, *The Everlasting Man* (New York: Dodd Mead, 1925), esp. 239–41.

21. Phillips, *Time of War*, 148.

22. For example, Beverslius, *Search*, 2nd ed., 117–18.

23. For this and other objections, see Lewis, "Modern Theology and Biblical Criticism," in *God in the Dock*, 152–66.

24. For example, see Beversluis, *Search*, 2nd ed., 132–33.

25. *MC* 2:3. And see "What Are We to Make of Jesus Christ?," in *God in the Dock*, 156–60.

26. Wright, "Simply Lewis," *Touchstone*, March 2007, http://touchstonemag.com/archives/article.php?id =20–02–028-f.

27. McGrath, *A Life*, 226–27. Anthony Kenney, in "Mere C. S. Lewis" (a review of McGrath's *A Life* and *Intellectual World*, *Times Literary Supplement*, June 19, 2013, http://www.the-tls.co.uk/tls/public/article 1275683.ece), says that "Lewis's principal apologetic arguments have not worn well" and is dismissive of the trilemma and of Lewis's argument from desire but sympathetic to Lewis's general stance that "naturalism is collapsing under its own weight."

28. Horner, "*Aut Deus aut Malus Homo*: A Defense of C. S. Lewis's 'Shocking Alternative,'" in *C. S. Lewis*

as *Philosopher: Truth, Goodness and Beauty*, edited by David Baggett, Gary R. Habermas, and Jerry L. Walls (Downers Grove, IL: InterVarsity Press, 2008), 68–84, citing (on p. 84) Lewis, "What Are We to Make of Jesus Christ?," in *God in the Dock*, 159–60.

29. Daniel T. Williams, "Lacking, Ludicrous, or Logical?: The Validity of Lewis's Trilemma," *Midwestern Journal of Theology*, Spring 2012, 91–102; reprinted as chapter 4 of Williams, *Reflections from Plato's Cave: Essays in Evangelical Philosophy* (Lynchburg, VA: Lantern Hollow, 2012). A shortened and popularized version of this piece was published as "Identity Check: Are C. S. Lewis's Critics Right, or Is His 'Trilemma' Valid?," *Touchstone*, May–June 2010, 25–29.

30. Kreeft, *Fundamentals of the Faith: Essays in Christian Apologetics* (San Francisco, Ignatius, 1988), 59. Probably the most influential instance of popularizing and expanding the argument and associating it with Lewis is found in Josh McDowell's immensely popular *Evidence That Demands a Verdict* (San Bernardino, CA: Here's Life, 1979 [1972]), 104–5.

31. Michka Assayas, *Bono: In Conversation with Michka Assayas* (New York: Riverhead, 2005), 204–5. I am grateful to Larry Eskridge for this reference. He has also provided other "*Mere Christianity* sightings" in popular culture, such as an account of punk rocker Larry Chimes's conversion in response to Lewis's chapter on pride: Madeleine Teahan, "Punk Rocker Describes His Return to Catholicism," *Catholic Herald*, January 28, 2014, http://www.catholicherald.co .uk/news/2014/01/28/punk-rocker-describes-his -return-to-catholicism/. Orson Bean, in *Mail for*

*Mickey* (Fort Lee, NJ: Barricade, 2008), tells of striking interest in *Mere Christianity* in the world of television (8) and uses the trilemma argument (131).

32. *MC* 3:6.

33. *MC* 3:8.

34. *The Letters of Dorothy L. Sayers*, edited by Barbara Reynolds (Cambridge, England: The Dorothy L. Sayers Society & Carole Green, 1998), 3:375 and 4:144, as quoted in Mary Stewart Van Leeuwen, *A Sword Between the Sexes? C. S. Lewis and the Gender Debates* (Grand Rapids: William B. Eerdmans, 2010), 109–10.

35. Jacobs, *Narnian*, 252.

36. McGrath, *A Life*, 228–29.

37. Jacobs, *Narnian*, 255. See "Priestesses in the Church?" (1948), in *God in the Dock*, 234–39.

38. For instance, Ann Loades, in "On Gender," in *Cambridge Companion*, 160–73, does not mention *Mere Christianity*.

39. For an overview of debates on Lewis and gender, see the colloquium on that topic in *Christian Scholar's Review*, Summer 2007, 387–484, especially the introduction by Don W. King, which contains a bibliography (388–90). As in Van Leeuwen, these discussions typically have to do with the larger scope of Lewis's views of gender and women rather than debating his remarks in *Mere Christianity*, which are taken as dated and deplorable. A more recent collection is *Women and C. S. Lewis*, edited by Carolyn Curtis and Mary Pomroy Key (Oxford: Lion Hudson Press, 2015).

40. Van Leeuwen, *A Sword between the Sexes?*, 9–10. Margaret P. Hannay presented an early version of this observation in "Surprised by Joy: C. S. Lewis'

Changing Attitude toward Women," *Mythlore*, September 1976, 15–20.

41. Van Leeuwen, *A Sword between the Sexes?*, 109–38.
For examples of scholars' views of Lewis's misogynist remarks, see Van Leeuwen, *A Sword between the Sexes?*, 32. Kathryn Lindskoog, in her entry "Women" in *The C. S. Lewis Readers' Encyclopedia*, edited by Jeffrey D. Schultz and John G. West Jr. (Grand Rapids: Zondervan, 1998), 429, writes, "C. S. Lewis has often been accused of misogyny, but in truth his attitude toward women was generally enlightened." Cf. Will Vaus, *Mere Theology: A Guide to the Thought of C. S. Lewis* (Downers Grove, IL: InterVarsity Press, 2004), 142–43, for a similar argument.

CHAPTER EIGHT
Lasting Vitality of *Mere Christianity*

1. Dorsett, preface to *Lightbearer*, 9–10. John Stackhouse, in "Why *Mere Christianity* Should Have Bombed," *Christianity Today*, December 2012, 38–41, provides a valuable overview that takes into account some of the book's shortcomings while providing insights on its lasting strengths.

2. For instance, the popular Christian writer Lauren Winner remarks, "I read Lewis's *Mere Christianity* in high school. It was either given to me or I stumbled upon it; at any rate, I didn't really like it. One of the reasons I wrote *Girl Meets God*—and I think this is also one of the reasons spiritual memoir has been popular throughout the last decade—is that there are a lot of people who aren't asking the Enlightenment questions that more standard apologetics texts like

*Mere Christianity* strive to answer. Having C. S. Lewis, however brilliantly, explain the logic and rationality of Christianity didn't speak to me where I lived." Bill McGarvey, interview with Lauren Winner (ca. 2002), *Mars Hill Review*, http://www.marshillreview.com /menus/interviews.shtm. Sarah Arthur, citing Winner, observes that the "roadblock" for postmoderns may not be that Lewis is too modern but rather that he is "pre-modern." Arthur, "Roadblocks to Reading C. S. Lewis," presentation at C. S. Lewis Festival, Petosky, MI, October 2012. Arthur is, however, a sympathetic critic who suggests that people can get beyond such roadblocks, including Lewis's views on gender.

3. See Lewis, "The Funeral of a Great Myth, in *Christian Reflections*, 82–93.

4. Lewis, "Learning in Wartime," in *The Weight of Glory, and Other Addresses* (San Francisco: HarperOne, 1980 [1949]), 58–59.

5. Lewis, *The Screwtape Letters*, Letter 1.

6. The exception, of course, is gender, which he did not see as controversial in the 1940s but has proved to be. See my discussion in chapter 7.

7. Lewis, *The Screwtape Letters*, Letter 7. Cf. *Mere Christianity* 3:3, where Lewis says most of us have "the hope of finding support from Christianity for the views of our own party."

8. Eric Fenn said of the original draft of *Beyond Personality* that it gave "the impression of a purely individualistic approach." Fenn, however, was concerned to see more about the church or the Christian community rather than about politics. Fenn to Lewis, December 29, 1943, quoted in Phillips, *Time of War*, 238.

9. Lewis, "Learning in Wartime," 49 and 53.

10. *MC* 3:3.

11. *MC* 3:3.

12. Muggeridge, foreword to Michael D. Aeschliman, *The Restitution of Man: C. S. Lewis and the Case against Scientism*, rev. ed. (Grand Rapids: William B. Eerdmans 1988 [1983]), xi. See also Aeschliman's chapter "Common Sense and the Common Man," 2–15.

13. Lewis, *An Experiment in Criticism* (Cambridge, England: Cambridge University Press, 1961), 112.

14. *Times Literary Supplement*, September 17, 1954, 592, quoted in Hooper, *Guide*, 507.

15. Lewis, *Experiment*, 140. Hooper, in *Guide*, 522, points out the comparison with *Mere Christianity*.

16. *MC* 4:11.

17. Owen Barfield, introduction to Jocelyn Gibb, ed., *Light on C. S. Lewis* (London: Geoffrey Bles, 1965), xvi.

18. Barfield, "C. S. Lewis," in *Owen Barfield on C. S. Lewis* (Middletown, CT: Wesleyan University Press, 1989), 14. Barfield says this as though it applied to the whole of Lewis's income, not just to his royalties and fees. He also says that Lewis especially liked to help needy individuals that he heard about and sometimes corresponded extensively with them.

19. Lewis, "God in the Dock," in *God in the Dock*, 243.

20. CSL to John Beddow, October 7, 1945, *Letters*, 2:674.

21. Lewis, letter to the editor, *Christian Century*, December 31, 1958, 1515, in *Letters*, 3:1006–7.

22. *MC* 1:1.

23. *MC* 1:5.

24. This paragraph depends to a great extent on Joel D. Heck, who in "*Praeparato Evangelica*," in *Lightbearer*,

235–58, uses the same quotation (on p. 240), from *Voyage of the "Dawn Treader"* (New York: Macmillan, 1952), 75–76.

25. From Lewis, "Bluspels and Flalansferes" (1939), 265, quoted in Ward, "Good Serves the Better," 61–62; cf. 59–78. Cf. also my discussion in chapter 7. Ward exemplifies well the prevailing interpretations of Lewis on reason, emotion, and imagination.

26. See also my discussion of this point in chapter 7, drawing on Reppert's, *Dangerous Idea*. Lewis's "On Obstinacy of Belief," in *The World's Last Night, and Other Essays* (New York: Harcourt, Brace, 1960), is especially helpful on this point.

27. Austin Farrer, "The Christian Apologist," in Gibb, ed., *Light on C. S. Lewis*, 37, quotation from 31.

28. Holmer, *C. S. Lewis: The Shape of His Faith and Thought*, 8 and 86.

29. Packer, "Still Surprised by Lewis," *Christianity Today*, September 7, 1998, http://www.christianitytoday.com/ct/1998/september7/8ta054.html.

30. Lewis, *Surprised by Joy*, 138.

31. *MC* 3:10.

32. McGrath, *Intellectual World*, 136; cf. 129–146. Cf. McGrath regarding Lewis's argument from desire, 105–28. Scott R. Burson and Jerry L. Walls, in *C. S. Lewis and Francis Schaeffer: Lessons for a New Century from the Most Influential Apologists of Our Time* (Downers Grove, IL: InterVarsity Press, 1998), also provide helpful insights on Lewis's apologetic method.

33. Quoted in McGrath, *Intellectual World*, 83, from Lewis, "Is Theology Poetry?," in *Essay Collection and Other Short Pieces* (London: HarperCollins, 2000), 21.

34. Lewis, *Miracles* (New York: Macmillan), 109.

35. Lewis, *The Magician's Nephew* (London: Bodley Head, 1955), chapter 10.

36. Lewis, "The Weight of Glory," 31.

37. See Michael Ward, "Escape to Wallaby Wood: Lewis's Depictions of Conversion," in *Lightbearer*, 143–67, esp. 146.

38. James Como, *Branches of Heaven: The Genius of C. S. Lewis* (Dallas: Spence, 1998), 150, based on the Winger interview with Como (n.d.); cf. 140–66. On Lewis's rhetoric, see Gary L. Tandy, *The Rhetoric of Certitude: C. S. Lewis's Nonfiction Prose* (Kent, OH: Kent State University Press, 2009); cf. Tandy, who is appreciative but also provides some criticisms of Lewis's arguments and rhetorical techniques.

39. Ward, "Escape to Wallaby Wood," 151; cf. 143–57.

40. Maudlin, "The Perennial Appeal of C. S. Lewis," presentation at the C. S. Lewis Festival, Petosky, MI, October 2012. I am indebted to Maudlin for furnishing me with a typescript of this talk. The talk also suggested the format of the present chapter.

41. Chad Walsh, *The Literary Legacy of C. S. Lewis* (New York: Harcourt, Brace, Jovanovich, 1979), 205.

42. Ward, "How Lewis Lit the Way," *Christianity Today*, November 2013, 38. The Lewis quotations are from "Bluspels and Flalansferes," 265.

43. Lewis, "Bluspels and Flalansferes," 265, quoted in Lyle H. Smith Jr., "C. S. Lewis and the Making of Metaphor," in *Word and Story in C. S. Lewis*, edited by Peter J. Shakel and Charles A. Huttar (Columbia: University of Missouri Press, 1991), 9 and 21. Smith points out that this view reflects a sort of Christian

Platonism in Lewis, who sees reality as made up of images and shadows that point to higher realities. One can find similar idealism in many places in the Christian tradition, as in Augustine or Jonathan Edwards.

44. Lewis, "The Language of Religion," in *Christian Reflections*, 139–40.

45. Ibid., 140.

46. Lewis, *The Abolition of Man* (New York: Harper-Collins, 1974 [1944]), 2. Cf. Michael Ward, "Good Serves the Better," esp. 62. This is one of the most helpful summations of Lewis's use of reason and imagination.

47. Barfield, "The Five C. S. Lewises," in *Owen Barfield on C. S. Lewis*," edited by G. B. Tennyson (Middletown, CT: Wesleyan University Press, 1989), 122.

48. Lewis, "Bluspels and Flalansferes," 265.

49. Lewis, "Is Theology Poetry?," 117.

50. Quoted from a manuscript that Hooper titles "Early Prose Joy," in Hooper, *Guide*, 181–82.

51. Preface to the French edition of *The Problem of Pain* (1950), from a translation in Hooper, *Guide*, 297. Lewis also remarks, "Even when I feared and detested Christianity, I was struck by its essential unity," 296.

52. Ferry, "Mere Christianity: Because There Are No Mere Mortals; Reaching Beyond the Inner Ring," in *Lightbearer*, 169–90.

53. Maudlin, "The Perennial Appeal of C. S. Lewis."

54. *MC* 12:3.

55. *MC* 4:8, 4:9, and 4:11.

56. Meconi, "*Mere Christianity*: Theosis in a British Way," *Journal of Inklings Studies*, April 2014, 3–18. *Mere Christianity* quotations from 4:7. Paul Fiddes, in

"On Theology," in *Cambridge Companion*, 89–104, explores the centrality in Lewis's theology of being drawn into the life of the Trinity and looks at both the strengths and some of the theological ambiguities of the metaphors Lewis uses to describe how that happens. Particularly, he points out, as some earlier commentators have, that the idea that the transformation involves being not just "made" but "begotten" by God, though not without precedent, is hardly "mere" or "common" Christianity (93).

57. Lewis, "The Personal Heresy in Criticism," in Lewis and E. M. W. Tillyard, *The Personal Heresy: A Controversy* (London: Oxford University Press, 1939), 11.

58. Dallas Willard, *Living in Christ's Presence: Final Words on Heaven and the Kingdom of God* (Downers Grove, IL: InterVarsity Press, 2014), 26. Cf. Paul Holmer, who observed in *C. S. Lewis*, "It is the authority of someone who has found something out about this or that and who tells us not how he feels but the way things are" (108).

atheism (*continued*)
on Lewis's use of reason
and, 142; trilemma and,
147, 149
*Atlantic Monthly*, 78
Atonement, 34, 75
Auden, W. H., 73, 80, 81
Augustine: idealism and,
241n43; popularity among
American evangelicals, 124;
as a source for Lewis, 63,
139, 233n17; trilemma
traced back to, 145
*The Average Man: Broadcast
Talk* (Wright), 49

Babbage, Stuart Barton, 31, 32
Bacon, Leonard, 66, 67
Barfield, Owen: on chrono-
logical snobbery, 10, 154;
Lewis's charitable donations
and, 39, 164, 239n18; on
Lewis's self-knowledge, 164;
on Lewis's sense of the uni-
verse, 180; Marion E. Wade
Center and, 113; meeting
with The Inklings, 15; told
by Lewis that his fame
would quickly pass, 107–8
Barth, Karl, 74, 77
*Basic Christianity* (Stott), 107
Battle of Britain, 31. *See also*
the Blitz; Royal Air Force
(RAF); World War II
Baxter, Richard, 91–92

BBC (British Broadcasting
Corporation): banning
pacifists after fall of France,
26; censor of, 34; challenge
of religious broadcasting
on, 23–27; Dorothy Sayers's
radio play on, 50; *The Listener* published by, 40, 57,
207nn50–51. *See also* radio
talks for BBC
Beckwith, Francis, 129
*Between Heaven and Hell*
(Kreeft), 128, 148
Beversluis, John, 140–43, 144,
148, 169, 230n6, 230nn2–3,
231n8
"Beyond Personality" (fourth
set of talks), 52–57; audience reaction to, 57,
207n51; Fenn's response to,
238n8; surviving recording
of, 56, 138
*Beyond Personality* (third
paperback), 50, 56; American Catholic reviews of, 71–
72; American edition of, 66;
American evangelical re-
views of, 76–77; becoming
part of *Mere Christianity*,
90–91, 96; British Catholic
view of, 61, 71, 208n8; latest
printing as separate volume,
215n1; modern Christian
critique of, 64; preface to,
93; reviewed by *NYTBR*,

68; reviewed by *TLS*, 60; reviewed in *New York Herald Tribune Book Review*, 210n28; ridiculed by Orwell, 59

biblical inerrancy: conservative evangelicals and, 112, 115; fundamentalist belief in, 99, 100, 105; not held by Lewis, 83, 99, 105, 112, 220n34; Packer's affirmation of, 107; progressive Protestants alarmed about, 62–63

biblical scholarship: Lewis's lack of interest in, 63–64, 102–3, 112, 146; modern standards of, 62–64, 102–3, 146; of N. T. Wright, 122; trilemma and, 146; working-class people's skepticism and, 33

Bles, Geoffrey, 40, 49, 90, 215n1

the Blitz, 19–21, 23, 34. *See also* Battle of Britain; Royal Air Force (RAF)

Bob Jones University, 129, 217n13

Bonhoeffer, Dietrich, 124, 185

Bono, 149

born again, 119

*Born Again* (Colson), 119

Bright, Bill, 219n30

Britain, Christianity in: competing beliefs and, 32–33; evangelicals and, 106–7, 121–22, 123, 170; largely nominal, 24–25, 26, 28–29; membership of major denominations in 1940, 201n13; moral sensibilities despite lack of, 34; revival of religious interest in 1950s, 98–99. *See also* Anglican faith; responses to Lewis in Britain

*Broadcast Talks* (first paperback), 40, 49; American evangelicals and, 76; American title for, 65; becoming part of *Mere Christianity*, 90–91; modern Christian critique of, 64; passage eliminated from *Mere Christianity*, 89–90; predicted decline of interest in, 109; preface to, 93; reviewed in *TLS*, 60. See also *Case for Christianity* (Lewis)

*C. S. Lewis: A Biography* (Wilson), 231n10

*C. S. Lewis: A Critical Essay* (Kreeft), 128

*C. S. Lewis: Apostle to the Skeptics* (Walsh), 82–83

*C. S. Lewis: The Shape of His Faith and Thought* (Holmer), 110–11

*C. S. Lewis and the Church of Rome* (Derrick), 130

suggestions of, 52; recruiting Dorothy Sayers, 50; responses to Lewis's talks and, 58; second set of talks and, 38–39, 40, 41–42, 43; theological background of, 30; third set of talks and, 43, 46, 47

Ferry, Patrick T., 184

Fiddes, Paul, 242n56

Flewett, Jill, 45

forgiveness: Lewis on, 28, 47; of sins by Jesus, 95

Forman, Henry James, 68

Frazer, James George, 6, 59

*Freethinker*, 58–59

Fremantle, Anne, 71

Freud, Sigmund, 156

Fryling, Bob, 114

*Fundamentalism and the Word of God* (Packer), 107

fundamentalists: American conservative evangelicals designated as, 75, 101; BBC policy excluding, 26; biblical literalism and, 83, 99, 100, 105 (*see also* biblical inerrancy); Lewis compared with, 82, 83, 100; Nott's critique of Lewis and Sayers as, 98; welcoming Lewis as an ally, 100, 114–15, 217n13; Wheaton College and, 104–5. *See also* evangelicals

gender and women, 48, 149–52, 237n41

Gibbon, Edward, 12

God, Lewis on belief in, 22, 89–90

*God and the Reach of Reason* (Wielenberg), 232n13

*God in the Dock* (Lewis), 110

*God Is Not Great* (Hitchens), 136–37

Golden, Edward A., 66

*The Golden Bough* (Frazer), 6, 59

grace, cheap, 185–87

Graham, Billy, 98–99, 100–102; building international evangelical networks, 106–7; in launch of *Christianity Today*, 105; Lewis's encounter with, 101, 107, 217n14; Lewis's perceived link to, 98–99, 101–2; Tom Phillips's conversion and, 117; Wheaton College and, 104, 113

*The Great Divorce* (Lewis), 77–78, 213n2

Great Sin of pride: *Christian Behavior* on, 47, 117–18; Chuck Colson's conversion and, 118; giving up the self and, 186; Lewis's comment about women and, 150; Monaghan's life changed by passage on, 127; Mormons' in harmony with

colleagues, 80–81; tutoring of students and, 15; understanding common human experience and, 111, 160–62, 165; wide study in, 10. *See also* analogy, Lewis's use of; metaphor, Lewis's use of

logic: Beversluis's criticism of Lewis based on, 140–41, 143, 230n6; Lewis's skill in, 88; Wielenberg on Lewis's arguments and, 232n13. *See also* reason

Longenecker, Dwight D., 128–29, 130–31

Lord Haw-Haw, 34

*The Lord of the Rings* (Tolkien), 15, 51, 137

*Los Angeles Times*, 81

Lowell, Virginia, 212n39

Luce, Henry, 80

Lu Xun, 135

MacDonald, George, 10, 113

Macmillan (American publisher), 49–50, 65–66, 90, 215n1

*The Magician's Nephew* (Lewis), 173

mainline Protestants, American: battled by fundamentalists, 75; fundamentalist embrace of Lewis and, 114–15; Holmer's late interest in Lewis, 110–11; "new

evangelicals" seeking cooperation with, 101; Pittenger's response to Lewis in 1950s, 101–6, 216n11; responses to Lewis in 1940s, 72–74, 82. *See also* liberal theologies; modern Christians of Lewis's time

making vs. begetting, 77, 242n56

"The Man Born to Be King" (Sayers), 50

Marion E. Wade Center, 113, 120, 153

marriage, Lewis's chapter on, 48, 95–96, 149–50

materialism, 12, 32, 75, 89, 170–71, 173

Maudlin, Mickey, 177–78, 184–85

McDowell, Josh, 235n30

McGrath, Alister, 123, 147–48, 150–51, 171–72, 234n18

Meconi, David, 186

*Mere Apologetics* (McGrath), 123

mere Christianity: Catholic resistance to, 132, 224n28; double meaning of, 181–82; Kreeft's exposition of, 128; lasting vitality of *Mere Christianity* and, 181–85; Lewis on meaning of, 40–41, 91–93; meaning unity despite differences, 131–32, mere Christianity (*continued*) 225n35; not minimal Christianity, 185. *See also* traditional Christianity of Lewis

*Mere Christianity* (Lewis): Beversluis's sustained attack on, 139–43, 144, 148, 169, 230n6, 230nn2–3, 231n8; changes compared to original three books, 95–96, 189–91; conversions influenced by, 116–21, 221n8; editions and printings of, 90–91, 97, 98–99, 215n1, 219n32; influence among evangelicals, 111–12, 114, 115; italics for emphasis removed from, 70; on moral principles common to cultures, 167; new preface to, 91, 93–95, 111; nonsectarian message of, 125, 182, 184; Pittenger's progressive critique of, 102–3; *The Problem of Pain* as anticipation of, 16–17; as repackaging of three earlier books, 2, 90–91; roadblocks to, for postmoderns, 237n2; sales of, 1, 2, 97, 108, 116, 135, 215n1, 217n19, 220n1; Stott's praise for, 107; translations of, 1, 134–36, 227n42; unobtrusive among author's

works, 97. *See also* lasting vitality of *Mere Christianity*; responses to Lewis in America; responses to Lewis in Britain

metaphor, Lewis's use of, 176, 178, 179, 180, 186, 242n56

Millet, Robert, 133

*Mind of the Maker* (Sayers), 50

Minto (Janie Moore), 7–9, 17, 44–45, 86–87

*Miracles* (Lewis), 78, 85–86, 88–89, 90, 172, 231n8

modern Christians of Lewis's time: beliefs of, 13; Lewis's stance in relation to, 83, 91–92; reacting to the radio talks, 61, 62–65. *See also* liberal theologies; mainline Protestants, American

*Modern Churchman*, 63–65

modern thought: of Lewis's radio audience, 165–66; subverted hopes of, 157. *See also* science

modern thought, Lewis's critique of, 154–55; loss of imagination and, 179–80; materialism and, 75, 89, 170–71, 172–73; moral education and, 51, 158; worldliness and, 174

Monaghan, Thomas S., 127

*Moody Monthly*, 75

Moore, Janie. *See* Minto (Janie Moore)

Moore, Maureen, 7, 8, 17

Moore, Paddy, 7–8

moral principles: *Abolition of Man* and, 51, 78, 158, 166–67; in "Christian Behaviour" radio talks, 46–48; of Quaker Trueblood, 79; sensibilities of radio audience and, 34. *See also* right and wrong, objective; sexual morality, Lewis on

*More Christianity* (Longenecker), 131

Mormon interest in Lewis, 132–33, 226nn37–38

Morrison, Charles Clayton, 72

Morrison, Terry, 114

Moyle, Marsh, 227n41

Muggeridge, Malcolm, 161

Murrow, Edward R., 23

Myers, Edward D., 73

Narnia books: Anscombe debate and, 214n9; as argument against naturalism, 89; confrontation with guilt in, 168; imagination and, 163; Lewis's reputation and, 108, 137; *The Lion, the Witch, and the Wardrobe*, 13, 87, 113; modern scientific assumptions and, 173; Pittenger's mention of, 102; reality of evil and, 37; writing of, 86–87

Narnia films, 137

National Association of Evangelicals, 77

naturalism: biblical scholarship and, 146; dominating contemporary thought, 157; Lewis's critique of, 156, 234n27; Lewis's early uncritical acceptance of, 11; Lewis's supernaturalism and, 86, 88, 112; Narnia books as argument against, 89; trust in reason and, 231n8. *See also* science; supernaturalism of Lewis

NBC, presenting one radio talk, 55–56

neo-Thomism, 82

new evangelicals, 101, 105. *See also* Graham, Billy

*New Republic*, 68–70

*New Statesman and Nation*, 99

New Testament: historicity of, 112; Wright's scholarship on, 122. *See also* biblical inerrancy

*New York Times Book Review* (*NYTBR*): on *Beyond Personality*, 68; on *Christian Behaviour*, 67–68; on mid-twentieth century religious writing, 81; on *Screwtape Letters*, 66

prayer: of evangelical commitment, 118; Lewis on, 40, 56, 95

preconditionalism, 233n17

*A Preface to Paradise Lost* (Lewis), 51

pride. *See* Great Sin of pride

*The Problem of Pain* (Lewis), 16–17; American edition of, 65; Beversluis's criticism of, 231n8; personal remarks in, 8, 16; sales of, 217n19; Welch's response to, 23, 27

progress: myth of, exploded by war, 10; scientism and, 78, 155

Protestants, American. *See* evangelicals, American; mainline Protestants, American

Protestants, British: response to radio talks, 61–65

psychoanalysis, 47, 156

Purgatory, 126

Quaker theologian Trueblood, 79

radio talks for BBC, 2; charitable donations of fees from, 39, 164; final series of, 52–57; first series of, 35–38; initial arrangements for, 23, 27–28, 30; number of

listeners for, 48–49, 205n33; preparing for the audience of, 32–34; of religious broadcasters other then Lewis, 49; second series of, 38, 40–43; third series of, 43–44, 45–49

radio talks for NBC, 55–56

rationalism: college students of 1960s and, 109; Lewis's early conflicts about, 11, 170–71; Orwell's critique of *Beyond Personality* and, 59. *See also* reason; science

reality: Lewis's use of metaphor and, 178, 242n56; modern disenchantment of, 172–73, 174, 179; spiritual, 11, 173

reason: Beversluis's criticism of Lewis based on, 140–41, 143; consensus on Lewis's use of, 143–44; context of, 168–76; criticism of Lewis's view of, 90, 233n17; faith and, 85, 136; Lewis's conversion based on, 14; Lewis's rhetoric and, 64, 149, 176. *See also* rationalism

*The Reason for God* (Keller), 123

Reith, John, 24

Reppert, Victor, 142–43

responses to Lewis in America, 136

responses to Lewis in America
of 1940s, 65–83; Alistair
Cooke's denunciation, 68–
70, 73; by Catholic publications, 70–72; by conservative evangelicals, 74–77; by
mainline Protestants, 72–
74, 82; in mainstream press,
65–68, 77–83, 210n28; not
polarized as in Great Britain, 81–82; by Quaker
theologian Trueblood, 79
responses to Lewis in America
of 1950s, 99–107
responses to Lewis in America
of 1960s and beyond,
108–15
responses to Lewis in Britain,
136–38; of 1940s, 39–40,
47, 48–50, 57, 58–65; of
1950s, 97–99
Resurrection, 53, 143
revivalism: in America of
1940s, 75; of Billy Graham,
98, 101; Lewis and, 104, 105
rhetoric of Lewis: reason and,
64, 149, 176; skill in, 88,
141, 144
right and wrong, objective,
28, 36–37, 38, 141–42, 166–
68. *See also* moral
principles
Roman Catholic Church:
American Protestants with
prejudices against, 82; Bob

Jones University's opposition to, 129; British population belonging to, 26,
201n13; Lewis's sending
drafts to representative of,
40–41; Lewis's theological
difference from, 61, 208n8
Roman Catholics: American
admirers of Lewis among,
100; Colson's initiative between evangelicals and,
225n35; converts influenced
by Lewis, 125–29; criticism
of *Mere Christianity* by,
130–31, 132, 224n28,
225n30; influenced by
Lewis, 125–31; Lewis's
friendships with, 183–84;
literary figures influencing
Lewis, 11; reviews of Lewis's
work in 1940s by, 61, 70–
72, 76, 77. *See also* Kreeft,
Peter; Tolkien, J. R. R.
Royal Air Force (RAF):
Leonard Cheshire of, 126;
traveling lectures for, 31–32,
40, 51, 55, 84
Russell, Bertrand, 59

*The Saints' Everlasting Rest*
(Baxter), 92
salvation: Lewis's doctrine not
the Catholic view of, 61,
208n8; Lewis's early view
of, 13; in Lewis's

individualistic message, 99; Lewis's use of analogy about, 185; Stott on, 107

*Saturday Review*, 66, 67

Sayers, Dorothy: American evangelical embrace of, 113; becoming friend of Lewis, 50; on controversial reputation of Lewis, 65; Lewis's domestic issues and, 45; Lewis's RAF lectures and, 32; on Lewis's views about women, 150; as religious writer, 50, 81, 97–98; suggesting the writing of *Miracles*, 85

Sayers, George, 36

schools, British, Lewis's cultural critique of, 78, 158, 166–67, 180

Schumacher, E. F., 126

science: anti-Christian elements in the press and, 59; blinding people to moral realities, 168; British public's rejection of Christianity and, 29; humanism and cultivation of, 98. *See also* modern thought; naturalism

science, Lewis's disillusionment with, 156–57; "Great Myth" of modernity and, 154–55; after his conversion, 14; as not capturing meaningful experience, 178–79; as roadblock to spiritual reality, 11, 173; after World War I, 10, 16

scientism: Lewis's criticism of, 78, 83; Lewis's novelistic critique of, 15–16, 156

Scopes "Monkey Trial," 101

*The Screwtape Letters* (Lewis): American evangelicals and, 75, 104, 212n39; charitable donation of payments for, 39; complimented by Dorothy Sayers, 50; conception and publication of, 29–30; Driberg's critique citing, 99; first American edition of, 65; lauded by American mainstream press, 66; Lewis's personal struggles and, 163–64; Lewis typically known as author of, 97; "mere Christianity" mentioned in, 91; modern Christian critique of, 64; moral rationalizations and, 168; motion picture rights for, 66, 209n20; partisan politics tied to religion and, 158, 238n7; Quaker theologian Trueblood on, 79; sales of, 67, 108, 116, 210n21, 217n19; science and scientism in, 156–57; success of, 49, 50, 61–62

World War II (*continued*)
England and France, 17–18; fighting for Christian civilization and, 28, 38; traumatic to the British people, 19–22; United States drawn into, 44. *See also* Battle of Britain; the Blitz

Wright, N. T., 122, 147, 148

Wright, Ronald Selby, 49, 205n34